BUDGET
CELEBRATIONS

BUDGET
CELEBRATIONS

The Hostess Guide to Year-Round Entertaining on a Dime

by **SHELLEY WOLSON**

POINT*click*HOME

First published in 2009 in the United States of America by

Filipacchi Publishing

1633 Broadway

New York, NY 10019

PointClickHome.com is a registered trademark

of Hachette Filipacchi Media U.S., Inc.

Design: Beatrice Schafroth

Editor: Lauren Kuczala

Production: Lynn Scaglione and Annie Andres

ISBN-13: 978-1-933231-63-1

Library of Congress Control Number: 2009923649

Printed in China

Contents

INTRO

Who doesn't love entertaining, especially at the holidays? However, it's no secret that we're all feeling the pinch in our pocketbooks these days, and hosting a gathering can get expensive and stressful. No more! You don't have to spend a fortune to throw an impressive soirée. There's a solution right here at your fingertips!

In this book we offer a wide range of ideas to minimize the costs and maximize the fun. You can definitely be a generous host without breaking the bank. With just a few tweaks in your menu and some simple, low-cost decorating projects, you can still entertain in style.

If you follow the ideas in these chapters, I guarantee you'll be able to create a memorable fête your friends and family will be talking about for years to come. No one will ever know you hosted an event on limited funds, and you'll also have money left over for planning the next one. Best of all, you'll be able to relax and throw a great party that you can enjoy right along with your guests.

This collection of inspiring photos and easy-to-follow instructions gives you all the information you need to have a good time without straining your budget. You'll find delicious, efficient menus and recipes to amaze everyone, along with festive and elegant decorating tips and tricks to set the stage for every special occasion.

I hope you turn to this resource for every wonderful celebration to come. Happy entertaining!

—Shelley Wolson

CHAPTER 1

CAST A SPELL

Conjure up some fun on Halloween with these gothic and glamorous decorating ideas, easy and clever creepy crafts and wickedly delicious goodies. Whether you're aiming to involve your kids in a cute project or want to give friends and neighbors a sophisticated spooky welcome, these charming ideas are positively bewitching. Your guests will be captivated by your creativity and the enchanting magic and mayhem displayed inside and outside your home!

halloween *decor*

CREATE A FRIGHTFULLY
DELIGHTFUL FOYER
AND MAKE A HAUNTING
IMPRESSION, WITH BATS,
RAVENS AND PUMPKINS
LARGE AND SMALL

1. Treats to go

A banner beckons little ghouls to help themselves to mini–treat bags hung from a haunted tree.

2. Hanging out

A black paper skeleton-and-skull banner creates a spook-tacular scene, and can be viewed indoors and out.

3. Afraid of spiders?

Who wouldn't be scared of this gigantic tarantula? Picture-hanging wire helps display the enormous store-bought arachnid. He's coming down a spiderweb stretched from the roof.

4. Ultimate spiderweb

Spray-paint a Twig Wreath* black and cover with black glitter, then decorate with faux silver dollars and black tulle, and let a black-glittered spider dangle in the center of a window.

* For instructions, see p. 136.

Last-minute decor

Make streamers by cutting black garbage bags into strips and hanging them from doorways. Stretch cotton or Dacron batting over picture frames and in corners to create spiderwebs.

1. Ghostly gathering

Tatty Curtains* frame a scene of Pom-Pom Spiders* skittering across the floor, beneath a table laden with Perching Blackbirds* and glowing candles. Black construction-paper door Moldings* and other clever details make this the spookiest Halloween decorating scheme ever.

2. Bone china

Clean glass dishes and frightening fabric are all it takes to decoupage these shudderingly scary Skull Plates.* Group them on a wall to add ghoulish glamour, or give away as creepy party favors.

3. Bowlful of bugs

A decorative glass bowl is positively crawling with plastic Beetles,* spray-painted black and finished with a spritz of opalescent blue on their shining buggy backs.

4. Creepy collection

Skulls and statues and bell jars full of brains are the *objets* that make up this ghastly grouping. Haunt crafts stores and yard sales—or search your attic and closets—for funky, inexpensive props that can be pressed into service for a display. The scarier, the better!

* For instructions, see p. 136.

3. The birds

Perch fake black crows
on front porch lights
to set a macabre,
Hitchcockian mood.

1. Fright lights

Flickering candlelight
reflected in candy jars casts
a ghostly glow. Paint designs
on black candles using white
acrylic paint mixed with
candle painting medium,
which lets it stick to wax.

2. Scare tactics

Pumpkin votives cast a warm
glow on the face of this
pointy-headed ghost made
out of sheets and white
netting. Set out a ghostly
group on bamboo stakes with
wire "arms." Hang them from
trees in your yard so they can
billow in the wind.

4. Boo-tiful welcome

Playful pennants, store-
bought bats and an array
of pumpkins invite guests
to check their broomsticks
at the door and experience
a hauntingly good time.

halloween crafts

SAY BOO! CAPTURE THE
SPIRIT OF ALL HALLOWS'
EVE WITH QUICK AND
SIMPLE PROJECTS THAT
MAKE YOUR HOME TOO
CUTE TO SPOOK

1. Crafty cutouts

A little black magic turns automotive window tinting film into Spooky Shadows.* Draw a design with a white oil paint marker. Cut out along inside edges; apply film cutouts to windows.

2. Special effects

These Jolly Jack-o'-Lanterns* cast a jaunty glow. All it takes to make them is a few glass votives, some paper, glue and a talent for making faces.

3. Fright site

Candy spiders and ghosts hang out with craft-foam bats in this hauntingly cute Centerpiece.*

4. Goblin gang

Balloons, markers, double-stick tape and paper make this an easy, fun craft for little tricksters. Hang up the Gang of Ghoulies* with string or raffia.

Rooms with a boo

Clever indoor decor that you and your children create together can be reused for years of haunting celebrations. Focus on decorating areas in which guests will congregate and roam.

* For instructions, see p. 136.

1. Heart-felt friends

Skeletons and zombies do have a heart after all, as these Felted Dolls* attest. Our friendly zombie is knit from felt-friendly wool yarn, with button eyes and an embroidery thread smile, while the bone man is cut, stuffed and stitched from black and white felt. Both are cute enough to keep around after the trick-or-treating season is over.

2. No bones about it

Give yourself a Hand,* and spray-paint wooden balls and empty spools a skeletal shade of white. Carefully drill through the larger balls, glue together the "forearms," then string the rest of the pieces on sturdy yarn or twine to create these bony mitts that go *clackety-clack-clack* when you touch them.

3. Curl up by the fire

Sit, if you dare, in this cozy corner in the light of tall black candlesticks and a Construction-Paper Mantel* (use a copier to blow up our pattern to the desired size). The Black Cat Pillows* sport button eyes and white-thread whiskers—easy and cute—and they'll help you keep an eye on all those fuzzy spiders!

* For instructions, see pp. 136, 137 and 139.

1. All wrapped up

To make this Bandaged Guy,* use the pattern to transfer the bandages and other elements, and shape the image in pieces: first the gleaming eyeball, then working outward to the eye socket, cheeks, and finally the forehead and jaw, exposing that toothy grin.

2. Seasons greetings

Nothing says Happy Halloween like a Scary Hobgoblin,* all scowls and just looking for trouble. And this grinning prankster is one of our easiest jacks to tackle— just transfer the pattern, carve out the eyes, and finish with the jagged smile.

3. Pumpkin pizzazz

Carve out the words Tricks and Treats,* and tape colored construction paper behind the words to create a festive spotlight for your table, ready to be filled with…you guessed it.

4. Purr-fect pair

This Dirty Duo* requires a little caution when carving, but the scowling results are worth it! After transferring the patterns, start with the feline faces, then remove the background material from the top, bottom and left of the figures in sections, for better control.

* For instructions and pumpkin carving tips, see p. 138.

halloween *food*

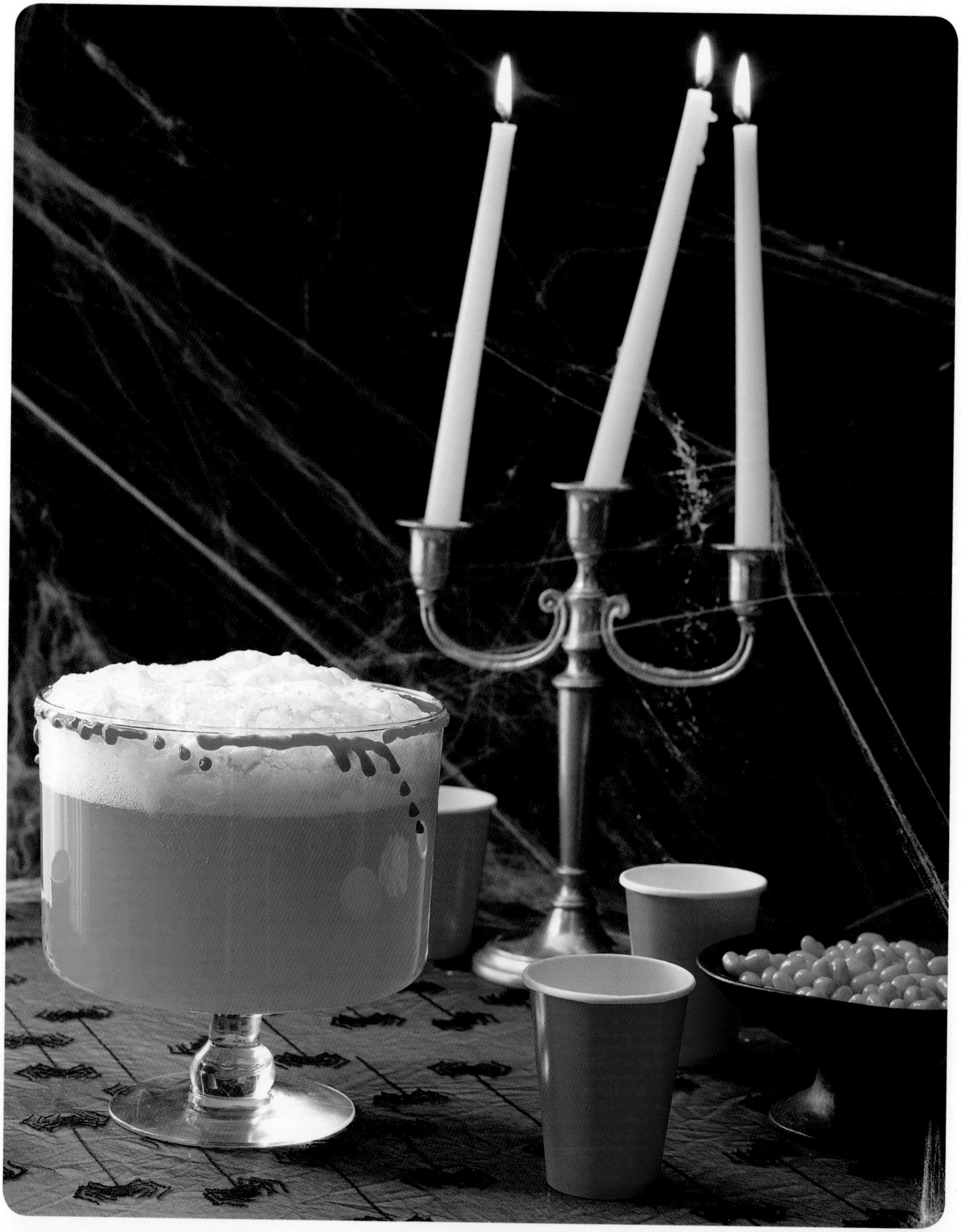

GUESTS WILL LOVE THIS MONSTER MENU OF GHOULISH GRUB THAT YOU'LL ENJOY MAKING WITH EASY-TO-FOLLOW, FUN RECIPES

MAKES ABOUT 36 BONES

PREP: 20 MIN
BAKE/SET: 4 HR

3   **cold large egg whites**

½   **tsp cream of tartar**

¾   **cup sugar**

1   **tsp almond extract**

Ground chocolate wafer cookies

WITCH'S
WICKED PUNCH

SERVES 12   MAKES ABOUT 3 QTS

PREP: 5 MIN   STIR: 1 MIN

Lemonade mix to make 1 quart

2   **tsp meringue powder**

3   **drops yellow food color**

6   **drops green food color**

1   **liter cold ginger ale**

2   **liters cold seltzer**

In an extra-large serving bowl, combine lemonade mix, meringue powder and food color. Gather your audience, then slowly pour in ginger ale and seltzer; stir to combine.

BAG OF BONES

1. Position racks to divide oven in thirds; heat to 225°F. Line 2 large baking sheets with nonstick foil.

2. Beat egg whites with cream of tartar in a large bowl with mixer on medium speed until soft peaks form. On high speed, gradually add sugar, a Tbsp at a time, and extract; beat 8 minutes or until stiff glossy peaks form and mixture no longer feels grainy.

3. Spoon mixture into a large ziptop freezer bag; snip off ¾ in. from one corner. Pipe bones of various sizes.

4. Bake 2 hours or until meringues feel firm. Turn off oven; leave meringues in oven 2 hours or overnight until crisp and dry. Peel off.

5. Arrange meringue bones on plate with cookie crumbs for dirt.

PUMPKIN PATCH BITES

1. Heat oven to 425°F. Line a rimmed baking sheet with nonstick foil.

2. On work surface, unroll pie crust and cut each of the two crusts into 12 pumpkin shapes with a 3-in. pumpkin cookie cutter. Using a 2-in. round cutter, cut 24 rounds from the sliced ham and 24 rounds from the sliced Cheddar.

3. Put 2 slices each ham and Cheddar in the center of each of 12 pumpkins. With a small brush, brush beaten egg around edges.

4. Top with remaining pumpkins, carefully pressing on edges to seal. Using a spoon, make ridges on pumpkins by pressing into tops in a few places. With a small knife, pierce ridges in a couple of places to vent.

5. Place on prepared pan. Brush tops with beaten egg. Bake 10 to 12 minutes until light golden. Let cool on rack a couple of minutes before serving.

MAKES 12

PREP: 30 MIN
BAKE: 10–12 MIN

1 **box (15 oz) refrigerated pie crusts**

6 **oz sliced Black Forest or Virginia ham**

8 **oz sliced extra-sharp Cheddar, Swiss or Gruyère cheese**

1 **large egg, lightly beaten**

Cookie Decorating 101

DECORATING COOKIES BEFORE BAKING

❖ Use decorations that withstand the heat, including: colored sugars; jimmies, nonpareils and a variety of shaped sprinkles; candy-coated chocolate and flavored baking chips; raisins and dried fruits; whole or coarsely chopped nuts.

❖ For better control, place sugar or sprinkles in a disposable decorating bag or parchment bag, then cut a small opening in the tip.

❖ Segregate candies, chips, dried fruit and nuts in a muffin pan or individual silicone baking cups to make it easy to reach in and pick up.

DECORATING COOKIES AFTER BAKING

❖ Use royal icing or confectioners' sugar icing, rather than buttercream, for a smooth, pretty shine.

❖ The most vibrant color comes from gel or paste icing colors, not liquid food colors.

❖ For best results, use a decorating bag and the "flooding technique": With medium-consistency icing, outline your cookie or decoration; allow to dry a few minutes until it "crusts," then use a thinner icing to fill in (flood) the outlined design. If outlining and filling in two different colors, allow the outline to dry longer to prevent bleeding.

❖ Add decorations to the iced cookie before it dries hard.

CREEPY COOKIE STACKS

1. Heat oven to 350°F. You'll need baking sheets.

2. Knead flour into sugar cookie dough. Roll out dough on lightly floured surface to $^3/_{16}$-in. thickness. Cut out cookies using cutter set. Place 1 in. apart on baking sheets.

3. Bake 8 to 14 minutes until lightly browned around edges. Remove baking sheets to wire rack to cool 5 minutes, then remove cookies to rack to cool completely.

4. Prepare Royal Icing according to directions included with meringue powder. To decorate jack-o'-lanterns, use icing tinted orange, green and yellow. Spread orange icing on pumpkin-shaped cookie. Spread green on stem. Spread yellow on eyes, noses and mouths. Let stand at room temperature to set. When set, stack eyes, noses and mouths on pumpkin bases.

5. To decorate spider webs, use icing tinted green, black, orange, red and white. Spread webs with green icing and spider body with black icing. Let set at room temperature. Meanwhile, pipe on spider legs using black icing in a pastry bag fitted with a #2 tip. Let set at room temperature. Pipe white web using white icing in a pastry bag fitted with a #2 tip. Pipe face and details on spider using red, orange and green icing. Let set at room temperature. When dry, set spiders on top of webs.

6. To decorate bats and moons, use icing tinted yellow, black, purple, orange, white and red. Spread yellow icing on moon-shaped cookies. Spread black icing on bat body. Outline wings in black. Let stand at room temperature to set. When set, spread purple icing on bat body and wings; pipe face on bat using orange, white and red icing in pastry bags fitted with #2 tips. Let set at room temperature. When dry, set wings on top of moons and bat bodies on top of wings.

MAKES ABOUT 10 COOKIES

PREP: DEPENDS ON SKILL LEVEL
BAKE: 8–14 MIN PER BATCH

½ cup all-purpose flour

2 tubes (16.5 to 18 oz) refrigerated sugar cookie dough

Wilton Meringue Powder

Orange, green, yellow, black, red, white, and purple Wilton Icing colors

You'll also need: Wilton Stackable Halloween Cookie Cutter set

HAUNTED GINGERBREAD COOKIE HOUSE

MAKES 1

PREP: DEPENDS ON SKILL LEVEL

1 Wilton Pre-Baked Cookie
   House Kit, assembled
   according to instructions

Candy and candy corn included
   in kit as well as additional
   regular candy and harvest
   corn for embellishments

Extra candy bat and ghost
   decorations

Other candy, as desired

Chocolate wafer cookies,
   crushed

Necco wafer candies

1. Prepare orange and black decorating icings included in kit according to instructions. Fill included decorating bags with black and orange icing. Spread black icing over roof with a small metal spatula. Using bag, pipe edge on roof. Attach candy corn, orange mini round candies and candy ghost decoration on roof with black icing.

2. Pipe some of the black icing on house to make windows and door. Using orange decorating icing, pipe edges of house, window panes and curtains. Attach an orange mini round candy as a doorknob. Using icing, attach bat to house and candy corn to bottom edge of house. Let icing dry.

3. Place house on plate or platter. Scatter chocolate wafer crumbs around house. Make a path using Necco wafers.

CHAPTER 2

A FEAST
FOR THE EYES
AND TABLE

Thanksgiving is coming, and it's time to gather together with family and friends and give thanks for all our blessings. It's also time to celebrate with turkey and all the trimmings, both edible and crafty. The all-American bird provides inspiration in the kitchen, and autumn offers rich colors and leafy inspirations for creating keepsake-worthy and simple decorating projects for table and room settings. Your guests will be thankful for your beautiful menu and decor!

thanksgiving
decor & crafts

A COMBINATION OF
FESTIVE FALL COLORS
WITH BRIGHT, EYE-
CATCHING DETAILS WILL
ENHANCE YOUR
AUTUMNAL DECOR

1. Scene stealer

A dramatic Thanksgiving Wreath* adorns a mirror or hangs over the mantel. Turn a simple grapevine into the scene-setting star of your harvest holiday decor plan with glitter, ribbon and Chinese lanterns.

2. Garland of gratitude

Our charming Thankful Garland,* made from Chinese lanterns and floral wire, encourages family and guests to express their gratitude for this bounteous holiday in writing, for all the world to see.

3. Festive candles

Delicate gold "skeleton leaves" add a festive touch of fall to ordinary white pillars—yet these Leaf Candles* are also appropriate for year-round use (especially if you choose different colors).

4. Light a vignette

Candles of all shapes and sizes are always perfect for holiday celebrations.

Autumn in style

Warm harvest colors and touches of drama create a showcase room that suggests the bounty of the season. A few high-impact crafts go a long way to set the stage for fall entertaining.

* For instructions, see p. 139.

1. Smart service

Set an autumnal table with harvest colors and a leafy motif. Combine these attractive Thanksgiving Napkins,* made with our all-purpose leaf stencil patterns, with Beaded Napkin Rings.*

2. Autumn leaves

This showpiece Leafy Table Runner* is made from wool felt cut into leaf shapes and sewn or glued together. It's easy to create and so beautiful you'll want to use it again and again.

3. Acorn collectible

Create Chair Place Cards* using gold parchment paper and the all-purpose leaf pattern, decorated with acorn ornaments and a swath of thin ribbon. Guests will definitely want to take these home as keepsakes.

4. All that glitters

These Falling Leaves* have a golden bead to provide weight at the bottom. They're hung from the window moldings to add sparkle to the occasion.

thanksgiving
food

TURKEY IS ALWAYS THE

CROWNING CENTERPIECE

OF THIS BOUNTIFUL

MEAL, ACCOMPANIED BY

DELICIOUS SIDE DISHES

AND CONDIMENTS

ROAST TURKEY

1. Heat oven to 325°F. You'll need a shallow roasting pan with rack. Remove giblets, neck and any fat from turkey body and neck cavities. Discard fat. Dry turkey thoroughly inside and out with paper towels.

2. Tie or clamp legs together. Twist wing tips under back. Brush skin with butter; sprinkle with salt and pepper.

3. Place breast side up on rack in pan. Insert standard meat thermometer (if not using an instant-read) into center of a thigh next to body (not touching bone). Add broth to pan.

4. Roast 3 to 3¾ hours, basting every 30 minutes with pan juices, adding more broth or water if pan seems dry. If breast gets too brown, cover loosely with foil.

5. About two-thirds through roasting time, untie legs so heat can penetrate body cavity.

6. About 1¼ hours before turkey should be done, start checking for doneness. When thermometer reads 180°F in thigh, remove turkey to a serving platter or carving board. Let rest (at least 30 minutes) before serving for juicier meat and easier carving.

SERVES 8 (WITH LEFTOVERS)

PREP: 30 MIN WITH OCCASIONAL
    TURKEY BASTING
ROAST: 3–3¾HR   REST: 30 MIN

- **1 whole turkey (12–14 lb), fresh or frozen, thawed**

- **1 Tbsp stick butter, melted**

- **½ tsp each salt and black pepper**

- **1 cup chicken broth**

Garnish: fresh herbs

MENU

- Roast Turkey with Easy Gravy and Cranberry Sauce

- Chesnut-Sausage Stuffing

- Caramelized Mushroom Tarts

- Mashed Potatoes with Cheddar & Chives

- Roasted Brussels Sprouts

- Sweet Potato & Pear Gratin

- Green Bean Casserole

- Apple-Cranberry Tart

- Pumpkin Pie

- Baked Fruit Compote

MAKES 8 CUPS

PREP: 10 MIN   ROAST: 1¼ HR
COOK: 1 HR 40 MIN

4   turkey wings (3–4 lb)

2   medium onions, peeled
     and quartered

1   cup water

8   cups chicken broth

2   medium carrots, cut in
     chunks

2   medium ribs celery
     (with leaves),
     cut in chunks

4   sprigs fresh thyme
     or 1 tsp dried

¾   cup all-purpose flour

2   Tbsp stick butter or
     margarine

1   tsp freshly ground
     black pepper, or to taste

EASY GRAVY

1. Heat oven to 400°F. You'll need a large roasting pan.

2. Put wings in pan; add onions. Roast 1¼ hours or until wings are browned.

3. Put wings and onions in a 5- to 6-qt pot. Add water to roasting pan and stir to scrape up any brown bits on bottom. Add to pot. Add 6 cups broth (refrigerate remaining 2 cups), the carrots, celery and thyme. Bring to a boil, reduce heat and simmer, uncovered, 1½ hours.

4. Remove wings. When cool, pull off skin and meat. Save meat for another use.

5. Strain broth into a 3-qt saucepan. Discard vegetables; skim off fat (see Tip).

6. Whisk flour into remaining 2 cups broth until blended and smooth.

7. Bring broth in saucepan to a gentle boil. Whisk in flour mixture and boil 4 to 5 minutes to thicken. Stir in butter and pepper. Serve (see Note), or pour into containers and refrigerate up to one week or freeze up to one month.

Tip: Refrigerate overnight so the fat that rises to the top can solidify and be easily removed.

Note: On Thanksgiving, you can skim fat from turkey roasting pan drippings and add drippings to the gravy.

Planning tip: Make up to one month ahead and freeze in an airtight container. Thaw two days in refrigerator. Whisk often while reheating in a saucepan.

CRANBERRY SAUCE

MAKES 4¼ CUPS

PREP: 10 MIN   TOTAL: 25 MIN

  2 **bags (12 oz each) fresh cranberries**

  2 **cups water**

1¾ **cups sugar**

1. Place all ingredients in a large saucepan and bring to a boil. Reduce heat and simmer 15 minutes or until most of the cranberries have burst.

2. Remove from heat. Cool slightly, then refrigerate, covered, up to 2 weeks.

1. LIME-JALAPEÑO VARIATION Stir ⅓ cup chopped cilantro, 2 tsp grated lime zest, 1 Tbsp lime juice and 3 Tbsp chopped jalapeño peppers into cooled Cranberry Sauce (add a little jalapeño hot sauce for more heat).

2. PEAR-GINGER VARIATION Stir 1½ cups diced, peeled fresh pears and ¼ cup chopped crystallized ginger into cooled Cranberry Sauce.

3. APRICOT-SPICE VARIATION Stir ⅔ cup chopped dried apricots, ½ cup chopped toasted pecans and 1 tsp pumpkin pie spice into cooled Cranberry Sauce.

CHESTNUT-SAUSAGE STUFFING

1. Heat oven to 250°F. You'll need a large rimmed baking sheet.

2. Spread bread on baking sheet. Bake 20 minutes, stirring once, or until dry. Transfer to a large bowl.

3. Meanwhile, cook sausage in a large nonstick skillet over medium-high heat, stirring to break up sausage, 5 minutes, or until no longer pink. Drain off and discard fat. Stir in onions, chestnuts (if using fresh), celery and butter. Cook 4 to 5 minutes until vegetables are crisp-tender. Add to bread.

4. Add chestnuts (if not using fresh), parsley, poultry seasoning and salt. Toss to mix well. Add broth; stir to moisten evenly.

5. Stuff neck and body cavity of turkey loosely (don't pack; stuffing expands slightly as it cooks). Put any remaining stuffing in a greased shallow baking dish. Cover and bake 30 minutes. Uncover and bake 15 minutes more until lightly browned. (Makes 12 cups.)

SERVES 8 (WITH LEFTOVERS)

PREP: 40 MIN   BAKE: 65 MIN

- 1 loaf (1 lb) sourdough or crusty Italian bread, torn or cut in ½-in. pieces
- 1 roll (12 oz) pork sausage
- 3 cups chopped onions
- 2 cups (about 10 oz) peeled fresh chestnuts (*see Note*), broken in large pieces (if using fresh, buy 1 lb, or use bottled, canned or dry-packed roasted, peeled chestnuts)
- 2 cups chopped celery (include some leaves)
- 1 stick (½ cup) butter
- ½ cup chopped parsley
- 2½ Tbsp poultry seasoning
- 1 tsp salt
- 1½ cups chicken broth

Note: To peel, cut an X on the flat side of 10 chestnuts with the pointed tip of a paring knife. Arrange in a circle on a paper plate. Microwave on high 10 to 20 seconds, until X starts to open and points curl. Meanwhile cut 10 more chestnuts. Replace hot nuts with fresh; microwave fresh while peeling the hot nuts (they're very hot, so wear disposable latex gloves). Repeat until all are peeled.

Planning tip: Peel and break up fresh chestnuts up to one week ahead; bag and refrigerate. Prepare stuffing up to two days ahead; bag and refrigerate. Stuff bird just before roasting.

TOM COLICCHIO'S CARAMELIZED MUSHROOM TARTS

SERVES 8

PREP: 20 MIN   COOK: 1 HR 10 MIN

- 2 large shallots
- 3 to 4 Tbsp extra-virgin olive oil
- 1 lb mixed wild and cultivated mushrooms, cleaned, trimmed and thickly sliced
- Kosher salt and freshly ground black pepper to taste
- 1 clove garlic, peeled and minced
- 1 Tbsp fresh thyme leaves
- ¼ cup sugar
- ¼ tsp sherry vinegar
- 1 to 1½ cups onion confit (*recipe follows*)
- 1 pkg (17.3 oz) frozen puff pastry

1. Heat oven to 375°F. You'll need eight ½-cup ramekins and a baking sheet. Wrap 1 shallot in aluminum foil and bake until it is soft, about 15 minutes. Remove the roasted shallot from the oven, let it cool slightly, then peel it and set aside. Peel and mince the remaining shallot.

2. Heat 1 to 2 Tbsp of the oil in a heavy skillet over medium-high heat until it shimmers. Add just enough mushrooms to cover the bottom of the pan in a single layer. Add salt and pepper, and cook, turning the mushrooms when they begin to brown, about 2 minutes. Add some of the minced shallots, garlic and thyme, and continue cooking until the mushrooms are tender, about 2 minutes more. Transfer the sautéed mushrooms to a plate, wipe out the skillet and repeat, cooking the remaining oil, mushrooms, garlic, shallots and thyme in batches.

3. Increase the oven to 425°F. Combine the sugar and 1 Tbsp water in a small saucepan over medium heat. Swirl the pan until the sugar has completely dissolved, then let the mixture boil, swirling occasionally, until the sugar caramelizes and turns nut brown. Swirl the sherry vinegar into the caramel, then remove it from the heat.

4. Pour the caramel into ramekins and allow it to cool for about 1 minute. Cut the roasted shallot into eight pieces. Place a piece of shallot in each ramekin, cover with sauteed mushrooms and top with onion confit.

5. Cut the puff pastry into circles slightly larger than the top of ramekins. Lay the pastry circles over the onion confit on top of ramekins and place ramekins on a baking sheet. Bake the tarts until the pastry is puffed and golden, about 20 minutes. Cool for 10 to 15 minutes, then carefully invert ramekins and unmold tarts onto plates or platter and serve warm or at room temperature. If mushroom mixture is sticky, gently release with fork and put on top of pastry circles.

MAKES 3 CUPS

PREP: 8 MIN   COOK: 60 MIN

- 2 Tbsp extra virgin olive oil
- 6 large onions, thinly sliced (about 12 cups)
- Kosher salt and freshly ground black pepper
- 1 cup chicken broth
- 2 Tbsp white wine vinegar
- 2 Tbsp fresh thyme leaves
- 4 anchovy filets, chopped (optional)

ONION CONFIT

1. Heat oil in a large deep skillet over medium heat. Add onions, salt and pepper. Reduce heat to medium-low and cook, stirring occasionally, until onions are very soft but not brown, about 30 minutes.

2. Add broth and vinegar and simmer, continuing to stir occasionally, until the pan is dry and the onions are golden, about 30 minutes more.

3. Remove from heat and stir in thyme leaves and anchovies (if using). Serve warm or at room temperature. Confit should be refrigerated and can be made one week ahead.

SERVES 8 (WITH LEFTOVERS)

PREP: 20 MIN   COOK: 25 MIN

- **4 lb baking potatoes, peeled and cut in 2-in. chunks**
- **1¼ cups (5 oz) shredded extra-sharp Cheddar**
- **½ cup chopped fresh chives**
- **½ cup reduced-fat sour cream**
- **⅓ cup ⅓-less-fat cream cheese (Neufchâtel)**
- **3 Tbsp stick butter**
- **1½ tsp salt**
- **¼ tsp freshly ground black pepper**
- **Toppings: crumbled cooked bacon and shredded Cheddar**

Planning tip: Can be prepared through Step 2 up to one day ahead; refrigerate. When reheating, stir in a little milk if potatoes seem stiff. Spoon into serving dish (microwave-safe if reheating in microwave) and heat.

MASHED POTATOES WITH CHEDDAR & CHIVES

1. Boil potatoes in a large pot in water to cover 25 minutes, or until tender when pierced. Scoop off 1 cup cooking water, then drain.

2. Return potatoes to pot, add cooking water and remaining ingredients, except Toppings, and mash.

3. Spoon into serving bowl; add Toppings. Makes 8 cups.

SERVES 8

PREP: 15 MIN   ROAST: 15 MIN

   1 **Tbsp olive oil**

   2 **tsp minced garlic**

   ½ **tsp salt**

   ¼ **tsp freshly ground
       black pepper**

   3 **tubs (10 oz each) Brussels
       sprouts, trimmed and halved**

   1 **tsp freshly grated lemon zest**

   1 **tsp lemon juice**

ROASTED BRUSSELS SPROUTS

1. Heat oven to 500°F. Line a rimmed 15 x 10-in. baking sheet with nonstick foil.
Mix oil, garlic, salt and pepper in a large ziptop bag. Add sprouts, seal and turn to coat.

2. Spread on prepared baking sheet. Roast 15 minutes, or until crisp-tender when
pierced. Sprinkle with lemon zest and juice; toss to coat.

Planning tip: Can be made through
Step 1 up to one day ahead. Roast just
before serving.

SERVES 8

PREP: 20 MIN   COOK: 20–25 MIN
BAKE: 15 MIN

3   **lb medium sweet potatoes**

3   **Tbsp stick butter**

2   **tsp grated peeled ginger**

⅓   **cup maple or pancake syrup**

1   **tsp grated lemon zest**

½   **tsp salt**

3   **firm-ripe Anjou pears
    (1¼ lb), peeled, halved,
    cored and sliced crosswise
    ¼ in. thick**

SWEET POTATO & PEAR GRATIN

1. Boil potatoes in a large pot with water to cover 20 to 25 minutes until firm-tender.
Drain in a colander; let stand until cool enough to handle.

2. Meanwhile, melt butter in pot. Add ginger; cook until fragrant. Remove from heat;
stir in syrup, lemon zest and salt.

3. Heat oven to 350°F. Grease a shallow 2- to 2½-qt baking dish.

4. Peel potatoes; slice ½ in. thick. Layer, alternating with pears, in baking dish
(microwave-safe if reheating in microwave). Brush with half the butter mixture.

5. Bake 15 minutes; brush with remaining butter mixture. Bake 15 minutes more,
or until pale golden around edges. Spoon juices on bottom of dish over top.

Planning tip: Can be made up to one
day ahead. Reheat in microwave, or in
oven if space permits.

SERVES 8

PREP: 20 MIN   COOK: ABOUT 13 MIN
BAKE: 30 MIN

2   lb fresh green beans, stem
    ends removed, beans cut in
    thirds *(see Note)*

2   Tbsp stick butter

1   cup thinly sliced shallots or
    chopped onion

10 oz baby bella mushrooms,
    sliced

4   oz shiitake mushrooms,
    stems twisted off and
    discarded, caps sliced

1   box (18.3 oz) creamy
    portobello mushroom soup
    (we used Campbell's Select)

1   can (2.8 oz) French-fried onions

GREEN BEAN CASSEROLE

1. Heat oven to 350°F. Lightly coat a 2-qt shallow baking dish with nonstick spray.

2. Bring a 4- to 5-qt pot of lightly salted water to a boil. Add beans; cook 7 to 8 minutes until crisp-tender. Drain and return to pot.

3. Meanwhile, melt butter in a large nonstick skillet over medium-high heat. Add shallots and mushrooms; sauté 5 minutes, or until lightly browned and liquid from mushrooms evaporates. Add to beans. Pour on soup and toss gently to coat; transfer to baking dish.

4. Top with French-fried onions. Bake 30 minutes, or until hot and bubbly and onions are crisp.

Note: Instead of fresh green beans, you can use 2 lb (12 cups) frozen beans, cooked.

Planning tip: Can be prepared through Step 3, covered and refrigerated up to one day ahead. Bring to room temperature before baking.

APPLE-CRANBERRY TART

SERVES 8

PREP: 25 MIN
BAKE: 30 MIN   WARM: 5–8 MIN

- 1 refrigerated ready-to-bake pie crust (from a 15-oz box of 2)

- 3 medium Granny Smith apples, peeled

- ½ cup canned whole-berry cranberry sauce

- ¼ cup granulated sugar mixed with ¼ tsp each ground cinnamon and nutmeg

- 1 Tbsp butter, cut in small pieces

- Confectioners' sugar

1. Heat oven to 425°F. You'll need a baking sheet.

2. Unroll or unfold pie crust directly on baking sheet. With rolling pin, roll dough to a 12-in. round. Edges can be uneven.

3. Cut each apple in half. Remove core (a melon baller works well); turn halves cut sides down and slice thin.

4. Leaving a 2-in. border, arrange apples in a circle on pie crust, slightly overlapping. Pile remaining apples in center. Dot with cranberry sauce in 7 or 8 places. Sprinkle apples with sugar-spice mixture; dot with butter. Fold pastry border over apples.

5. Bake 15 minutes, then reduce oven temperature to 375°F and bake 15 minutes longer or until apples are tender and pastry is golden. Cool completely on sheet on a wire rack or slide off sheet onto serving plate if not rewarming.

6. To warm before serving: Heat tart in a 400°F oven 5 to 8 minutes. Dust with confectioners' sugar.

Planning tip: The tart can be baked up to one day ahead. Cool completely, cover and refrigerate on baking sheet if rewarming to serve. To serve warm, heat in 400°F oven 5 to 8 minutes.

PUMPKIN PIE

SERVES 8

PREP: 10 MIN   BAKE: 1 HR

- **1   refrigerated ready-to-bake pie crust (from a 15-oz box of 2)**

FILLING

- **1   can (15 oz) 100% pure pumpkin**
- **1½   cups milk**
- **¾   cup sugar**
- **2   large eggs**
- **2   Tbsp all-purpose flour**
- **2   tsp ground cinnamon**
- **½   tsp ground nutmeg**
- **¼   tsp salt**
- **Pinch each ground cloves and ginger**
- **Leaf decoration (see Note)**

1. Heat oven to 350°F. Fit crust into a 9-in. pie plate. If desired, crimp or flute edges, or decorate as shown (see Note).

2. Filling: Put all ingredients in a large bowl and whisk, or beat with an electric mixer, until blended. Pour into crust.

3. Bake 1 hour or until a pointed knife inserted near center comes out clean.

4. Remove to a wire rack and cool 1 hour, or refrigerate.

Note: Form a ½-in.-high rim around edge of crust. Using a sharp knife, cut through raised rim at ½-in. intervals. Alternating, turn cut edges in and out from edge of pie plate. Score lines with blunt edge of a knife. Using a leaf-shaped cookie cutter, cut leaves from other piecrust in box. Brush with water; sprinkle with sugar. Bake on a baking sheet until golden. Place 3 in center of baked pie; add rest to servings.

Planning tip: Crust can be decorated as shown (see Note) up to one week ahead. Freeze until hard, then wrap and freeze again. Thaw before filling. Pie can be baked up to two days ahead. Refrigerate covered.

SERVES 8 (WITH LEFTOVERS)

PREP: 5 MIN   BAKE: 1 HR
CHILL: AT LEAST OVERNIGHT

½   **cup brown sugar**

1   **cup white or red wine**

16   **oz (2½ cups) dried apricots**

1   **cup pitted prunes**

1   **can (20 oz) pineapple chunks
     in juice, not drained**

1   **can (21 oz) cherry pie filling**

BAKED FRUIT COMPOTE

1. Heat oven to 350°F. You'll need a 2- to 2½-qt shallow baking dish.

2. Dissolve sugar in wine. Put dried and canned fruits in baking dish, add wine mixture and stir to mix. Cover with foil.

3. Bake 1 hour, or until most of the liquid is absorbed. Uncover, cool and transfer to serving dish; cover and refrigerate overnight.

4. Serve cold or at room temperature.

CHAPTER 3

COMFORT
AND JOY

The pleasures of the holidays are many, the greatest being entertaining family and friends. This year keep everyone's spirits bright by decorating simply and planning ahead for meals. From quick-to-make table appointments and tastefully matching color details to delicious and beautiful food, it will be easy to ratchet up the visual impact without spending a fortune. Best of all, you can involve the whole family in the magic of the season.

christmas
decor

CREATE A SPARKLING

RED-AND-WHITE

DECORATING THEME TO

SPREAD HOLIDAY CHEER

INTO EVERY ROOM IN

THE HOUSE

4. Fresh forms

Antique candleholders prop up Topiary Balls* made of red pistachio nuts glued to plastic-foam forms, while apples attached to a cone-shaped form create a topiary tree atop a glass compote. Red holiday candies in a glass vase finish the effect.

1. Merry and bright

A single color scheme unifies a room. Sew a Tree Skirt* of charming red crewel-like fabric, craft an array of complementary tree ornaments and use color-appropriate accessories, such as bright pillows, tablecloths and ribbons.

2. It's a wrap

Gifts wrapped in brown kraft paper and embellished with ribbon, raffia and rickrack become part of the decor. Include a gala mix of striped, checked and solid-colored ribbons, dried flowers, felt snowflakes, buttons or berries for extra pizzazz.

3. Special spheres

Scour crafts and home stores for woodland-like spheres to display with seasonal trimmings and gatherings.

Inspired design

Use your imagination to carry out the theme. Try filling an empty wall with a handsome wreath adorned with red ribbon to tie everything in.

* For instructions, see p. 140.

1. Stocking display

A jazzy Parade of Stockings* enriches the mantel, which is festooned with a Pinecone Garland.* Tiny packages in similar colors peeking out of the stockings increase the vignette's charm.

2. Personal touch

Personalized napkin rings are special. Loop twisted embroidery floss or yarn around napkins and secure at the back with florist's wire or a simple knot. Then add leaves and berries and inscribe names with silver paint or metallic pens.

4. Sweet sensations

Small brown candy bags chockful of peppermints and dressed with spunky ribbons are thoughtful giveaway gifts. Don't forget to include tags with a "Merry Christmas" greeting.

3. Eye candy

Top a sideboard with a bundle of holiday blooms set in a Candy Cane Container* that fits the occasion. Glued-on bands of scarlet ribbon add a pretty touch.

* For instructions, see pp. 140 and 141.

christmas *crafts*

DECK THE HALLS WITH

DETAILS THAT SHOUT

GOOD TIDINGS TO ALL

WHO VISIT. YOUR FAMILY

WILL LOVE MAKING

THESE KEEPSAKES, TOO

1. Thoroughly modern

Warm up the holidays with a totally contemporary take on red and green. This White Birch Wreath* is bundled in scarlet-and-pistachio-hued berries and set off with a pretty sage-colored bow.

2. Scrapbook

Decoupage photos from Christmases past onto ornaments and tuck them into a Memory Wreath* to take pride of place on a wall, a window or your front door.

3. Gift giving

The whole family can contribute to the Gift Box Wreath,* which repurposes gift-wrapping scraps and boxes in a playful design.

4. Natural beauty

Abloom with dried hydrangeas, roses and pomegranates, this Hydrangea Wreath* ushers in the season.

Winter welcome

Nothing says Christmas like a beautiful wreath. But don't stop with just one—adorn your doors inside to create an even warmer holiday welcome.

* For instructions, see pp. 141 and 142.

1. Brilliant baubles

Why should the tree get all the attention? Set aside your most fragile and beautiful ornaments for display around the house. Place a footed bowl filled with ornaments in your entryway for a dazzling first impression.

2. Glamorous glow

Nothing says Christmas quite like candlelight. Place a pillar candle in the center of a glass vase and fill in the empty space with pretty balls. Put the vase on a tabletop or on your mantel for a special festive glow.

4. Perfect package

Whether you've run short of boxes or just want to try something new, here's a quick and clever gift-wrap solution for soft items like sweaters and throws. First wrap your gift with tissue paper, then add a layer of colored corrugated cardboard (available at crafts stores). Tie on a ribbon and a handwritten name tag for a finished look.

3. Lovely linens

Make your dining table shine with this elegant napkin ring. Pick up clear crystal prisms from a crafts store and tie them around tightly rolled napkins with ribbon or twine. Display in a bowl on your buffet.

3. Swirls of color

A paintbrush, some glue, colored glitter and lots of imagination are all it takes to make Swirly Ornaments,* destined to become keepsakes year after year.

4. Stunning jewels

Give a second life to old glass ornaments that have lost some of their luster. Glue shining faux gems of all sizes to plain colored globes to create one-of-a-kind Rhinestone Ornaments.*

1. Beautiful birds

We added a cascade of pretty white feathers for a dramatic flourish to Holiday Doves.* Well-stocked crafts and holiday stores carry every type of faux birds, so select the ones you like the best.

2. Nature's sparkle

Ordinary baubles are transformed into Nature's Ornaments* with a coat of thin glue and a roll through colorful glitter. Finish by attaching tiny glittered ladybugs or other decorations with an additional dab of glue.

5. Floral arrangement

Faceted acrylic jewels hot-glued to a delicate golden ring create sparkling Crystal Flower Napkin Rings.*

* For instructions, see p. 142.

1. Crafty cards

An easy way to personalize your store-bought cards is to dress them up with ribbon and other shimmery trimmings. Gather beads, sequins and metallic ribbon, and attach them to cards using a clear all-purpose adhesive such as Awesome Glue.

2. Bag it

Cut a festive pattern—front and back pieces, two sides, a bottom and a handle—from rosy felt to craft a nifty Yuletide Gift Bag.* Sew the pieces together either by hand using a blanket stitch or by machine. Pop in some snowflake-white tissue to keep homemade food gifts like cookies or fruitcake safe and sound for carrying.

3. Foot warmer

At the front door, a Stocking Doormat* embellished with a cheery red-and-green-striped design practically shouts, "Good tidings one and all!" Hefty boots and a snappy coat left outside—evidence of Santa's visit—will enchant your company!

4. Pitter-patter

Give all those socks that have lost their mates a Christmas role. Dyed red, the different shapes heighten the fun of a Noel Garland.* Spruce up each sock with a fetching button or bow. Then, glue or sew the whole bunch to a bright red ribbon. Yesterday's big red stockings, filled with stuffing and sewn shut, make super-comfy Floor Pillows* to cuddle during story time.

* For instructions, see pp. 142 and 143.

christmas *food*

USE THIS SEASONAL

SELECTION OF GREAT

CROWD-PLEASING

RECIPES TO MAKE EVERY

HOLIDAY GATHERING

MEMORABLE

FANCY POTATOES

MAKES ABOUT 50

PREP: 15 MIN   COOK: ABOUT 20–25 MIN

- 1 **bag (about 1½ lb) mixed baby potatoes**
- 1 **container (16 oz) reduced-fat sour cream**
- 1 **jar (2 oz) black, red, yellow or orange caviar**

Garnish: chopped chives (optional)

1. Bring a large pot of water to a boil. Add potatoes and cook until tender when pierced with the tip of a knife, about 20 minutes. Drain and cool.

2. Cut each potato in half and cut a small slice from the bottoms so they will sit flat. With a small spoon, scoop out some of the potato. Fill potatoes with a dollop of sour cream. Top with caviar. Arrange on a serving platter. Garnish with chives if desired.

NEW TRADITION

Try throwing an appetizer party this holiday season! Host an event where you serve a wide variety of bite-size choices for guests to nibble on throughout the evening. It's a great, low-cost alternative to a traditional sit-down dinner. Make it potluck and you'll really stay within your budget, while showcasing everyone's special dish or favorite family tradition. Take it a step further and make it similar to a cookie swap: Have guests bring copies of their recipes to share along with their dishes!

Fun and festive

Trying to plan the perfect celebratory meal without breaking the bank? Often the holidays become stressful as we start thinking of all the food we have to buy, along with all the gift shopping. Don't stress! Pull together a simple menu ahead of time and stick to it, and make sure to let everyone help you prepare it.

MAKES ABOUT 24 SLICES

PREP: 15 MIN

- 4 oz ⅓-less-fat cream cheese (Neufchâtel)
- 2 Tbsp horseradish mayonnaise
- 2 each burrito-size (about 8 in.) sun-dried tomato flour tortillas and spinach flour tortillas
- 8 oz thinly sliced roast beef
- 2 scallions, cut in thin, long strips
- 4 matchstick-thick pieces seedless cucumber, cut 8 in. long

SLICED NEGAMAKI WRAPS

1. Mix cream cheese and horseradish mayonnaise until blended; spread on tortillas to within ½ in. of edges.

2. Divide roast beef; place on bottom two thirds of each tortilla. Top with scallion and cucumber near bottom edge. Starting at bottom, tightly roll up each tortilla.

3. To serve: Cut ends off tortillas. Then cut diagonally in 1-in.-thick slices (you'll get between 5 and 6 slices per tortilla).

Planning tip: Can be prepared through Step 2 up to 4 hours ahead. Wrap each in plastic wrap and refrigerate.

MAKES 50 MEATBALLS

PREP: 20 MIN   COOK: 20 MIN
BAKE: 30 MIN

SAUCE

- 1 **cup pickled Italian vegetables, such as giardiniera, drained (reserve about ½ cup liquid) and finely chopped**
- 1 **cup unsweetened applesauce**
- 1 **cup water**
- 1 **can (8 oz) tomato sauce**
- ¾ **cup packed light brown sugar**

MEATBALLS

- 2 **lb ground meat (beef, turkey, veal or a combination)**
- 2 **large eggs, lightly beaten**
- 1 **medium onion, minced**
- ½ **cup dried plain bread crumbs**
- ¼ **tsp cayenne pepper**

SWEET & SPICY MEATBALLS

1. Sauce: Place sauce ingredients, including reserved liquid, in large saucepan and bring to a boil over medium-high heat, stirring occasionally. Reduce heat to low and simmer 20 minutes or until slightly thickened.

2. Meatballs: While sauce simmers, mix meatball ingredients in a large bowl until well blended. Form into small balls (a slightly rounded tablespoonful) or use a level cookie scoop.

3. Heat oven to 350°F. Spray bottom of roasting pan. Arrange meatballs in single layer. Bake for 10 minutes. Turn meatballs over, then spoon over sauce. Cover pan with foil and bake 20 minutes more.

4. Stir lightly in pan before serving. Transfer to a serving bowl.

PECAN-JAM STARS

1. Toast nuts in a 350°F oven 5 to 7 minutes until fragrant. Cool.

2. Pulse nuts and ¼ cup flour in food processor until nuts are finely ground. Whisk nut mixture, remaining flour and salt in a bowl to combine.

3. Beat butter, sugar and vanilla in a large bowl with mixer on medium speed to blend. On low speed, beat in the flour mixture. Divide dough equally in fourths; roll each portion with a rolling pin between sheets of wax paper to ¼ in. thick. Slide dough onto baking sheets, stacking sheets of dough. Chill 30 minutes or until firm.

4. Heat oven to 350°F. Peel top paper off 1 sheet of dough. Cut stars with floured 2-in. star cookie cutter. Place 1 inch apart on baking sheets. Press scraps together and refrigerate.

5. Bake 8 to 10 minutes until lightly golden at edges. Cool slightly on sheet on a wire rack, then transfer to rack to cool completely.

6. Repeat with another sheet of dough. Transfer to baking sheet; with floured 1-in. star cookie cutter, cut out centers. Carefully remove centers; add to scraps.

7. Bake and cool cutouts as above.

8. Repeat with remaining dough.

9. To assemble, gently spread a scant teaspoon jam on each whole cookie. Top with the star cutouts; dust with confectioners' sugar.

MAKES 50

PREP: 40 MIN   BAKE: 20 MIN

- ⅔ **cup pecan halves**
- 3 **cups all-purpose flour**
- ½ **tsp salt**
- 3 **sticks (1½ cups) unsalted butter, softened**
- 1¼ **cups confectioners' sugar, plus extra for dusting**
- 2½ **tsp vanilla extract**
- ½ **cup each seedless red raspberry jam and apricot jam**

Storage tip: Refrigerate filled cookies airtight in a single layer up to 1 week; unfilled, freeze up to 3 months.

MAKES ABOUT 7 LARGE AND 25 SMALL

PREP: 40 MIN (WITHOUT DECORATING)
CHILL: 4 HR   FREEZE: ABOUT 25 MIN
BAKE: 17–19 MIN FOR LARGE COOKIES,
13–15 MIN FOR SMALL

5½ **cups all-purpose flour**

1½ **Tbsp ground ginger**

2 **tsp ground cinnamon**

1 **tsp baking powder**

½ **tsp each ground cloves,
    nutmeg and salt**

¼ **tsp baking soda**

2 **sticks (1 cup) unsalted butter,
    softened**

1 **cup light molasses**

½ **cup each granulated sugar
    and packed brown sugar**

2 **large eggs**

2 **tsp vanilla extract**

2 **Tbsp cider vinegar**

1 **cup Sugar in the Raw or
    coarse white decorating
    sugar**

ROLLED GINGERBREAD COOKIES

1. Whisk flour, ginger, cinnamon, baking powder, cloves, nutmeg, salt and baking soda in a bowl to blend.

2. Beat butter, molasses, sugars, eggs, vanilla and vinegar in a large bowl with mixer on medium speed to blend. On low speed, beat in flour mixture, 1 cup at a time, until a soft dough forms. Divide in thirds. Shape each third on plastic wrap into a 1-in.-thick disk. Wrap; chill 4 hours or until firm.

3. Lightly dust 1 disk at a time with flour (keep others chilled). Roll out between sheets of plastic wrap to ¼ in. thick for large cookies, ⅛ in. thick for small. Slide onto a baking sheet; freeze at least 15 minutes. Repeat with rest of dough, stacking sheets in freezer. Peel off top plastic wrap. Using floured cookie cutters, cut out cookies, leave on plastic and slide back on baking sheet. Reroll scraps and cut once. Freeze 10 minutes.

4. Heat oven to 350°F. Line baking sheet(s) with nonstick foil.

5. Place cookies 1 in. apart on lined baking sheet(s). Sprinkle with sugar.

6. Bake 17 to 19 minutes for large cookies, 13 to 15 minutes for small, until a bit darker. Cool slightly on sheet on a wire rack; move to rack to cool completely.

Storage Tip: Store airtight in a single layer at cool room temperature up to two weeks, or freeze up to three months.

ICING TIPS AND TRICKS

To cover a cookie with a smooth, flat coating of icing, add teaspoons of water to decorating icing until it is "flooding" consistency. To flood a cookie, outline cookie with flooding icing using a pastry bag fitted with a #2 or #3 pastry tip. Use the same tip to loosely fill in your outline, then spread icing evenly with an offset spatula or back of a spoon. To achieve a different texture, you can sprinkle sanding sugar, nonpareils or small dragées over the wet icing. To pipe over flooding icing, allow flooding to dry for 2 hours so flooding and decorating icings will not run together.

DECORATING ICING

3¼ **cups confectioners' sugar**

¼ **cup Just Whites** (see Note)

⅓ **cup water**

1. Beat sugar and Just Whites in a bowl with a mixer on low speed until combined.

2. Add water; beat until blended.

3. Increase speed to high; beat 8 minutes or until icing is very thick and white. Makes 2½ cups.

Note: You can find Just Whites (powdered egg whites) in your supermarket's baking supplies section.

GINGERBREAD CUTOUTS

1. Follow directions for Rolled Gingerbread Cookies, opposite. Using holiday-shaped cookie cutters, cut cookies out of dough. Chill, bake and cool according to directions.

2. For icing-covered cookies, use flooding method as described in Icing Tips and Tricks, opposite. To decorate plain or icing-covered cookies, fill a pastry bag with decorating icing fitted with a #2 pastry tip. Decorate cookies with lines and dots. Sprinkle wet icing with sanding sugar, dragées or nonpareils if more texture is desired. Let all dry for at least 2 hours.

FOREST OF TREES

1. Follow directions for Rolled Gingerbread Cookies, page 72, using large tree-shaped cutters. Chill, bake and cool cutouts according to directions. Save scraps in refrigerator for baking tree stands later.

2. For green trees, flood baked cookies with icing using method described in Icing Tips and Tricks, page 72, and allow to dry 4 hours or overnight. Mix ¼ teaspoon of green luster dust with enough drops of vodka to create a loose, paintlike consistency. Use a pastry brush or soft paintbrush to paint luster dust mixture on cookies. Allow to dry 1 hour before piping on additional decorations.

3. To decorate plain and green trees with garlands and baubles, fill a pastry bag with decorating icing fitted with a #2 pastry tip. Pipe lines for garlands, or dots for baubles. To create different colors and textures, sprinkle wet icing with colored sugars, nonpareils or dragées. Attach larger dragées to the peaks of trees with a dab of icing.

4. To make stands for trees, cut a triangle out of cardboard ½ to ⅔ the height of your trees. Trim triangle into an approximately 45-degree angle. Roll cookie-dough scraps to ¼ in. thickness; use cardboard as a stencil to cut triangles out of dough. Bake triangles, then attach onto the backs of trees with decorating icing. Allow to dry for 2 hours before setting trees into pattern on table.

COOKIE WREATH CENTERPIECE

1. Follow directions for Rolled Gingerbread Cookies, page 72. Using leaf-shaped cookie cutters, cut 35 to 45 leaves out of cookie dough. Use the back of a paring or table knife to draw veins in the leaves. Chill, bake and cool leaves according to directions.

2. To create centerpiece, arrange leaves in concentric, overlapping circles around a candlestick in desired location. Sift confectioners' sugar over cookies to create a snowy effect.

EGGNOG CHEESECAKE

1. Heat oven to 350°F. Coat an 8-in. springform pan with nonstick spray.

2. Crust: In a food processor, process cookies, hazelnuts and sugar until cookies and nuts are finely chopped. Add butter; pulse until blended. Press over bottom and 1½ in. up sides of prepared pan. Freeze until ready to fill.

3. Filling: Beat cream cheese, sugar, cornstarch and nutmeg in a large bowl with mixer on medium speed until smooth. Beat in eggs until blended, scraping sides of bowl twice. Beat in eggnog and rum. Pour into prepared pan.

4. Bake 45 minutes or until light brown around edges and center still jiggles. Turn oven off; leave cake in oven 1 hour.

5. Cool cake in pan on a wire rack. Run a long, thin knife between cake and pan sides. Refrigerate in pan at least 4 hours.

6. To serve, remove pan sides. Decorate top of cake with a border of Candied Cranberries and Sugared Rosemary.

Planning tip: The cake can be baked up to five days ahead. The Candied Cranberries and Sugared Rosemary can be prepared up to one day ahead.

SERVES 12

PREP: 25 MIN   BAKE: 45 MIN
CHILL: AT LEAST 4 HR

CRUST

- 20   shortbread cookies
- ¾ cup toasted hazelnuts
  (see Note)
- ¼ cup sugar
- 3 Tbsp cold butter,
  cut in small pieces

FILLING

- 3 bricks (8 oz each) cream cheese, softened
- 1 cup sugar
- 3 Tbsp cornstarch
- 1 Tbsp ground nutmeg
- 3 large eggs
- 1 cup canned or refrigerated eggnog
- ¼ cup dark rum

Garnish: Candied Cranberries and Sugared Rosemary
(see below)

Candied Cranberries: Bring ½ cup each cranberries, sugar and water to a boil in a medium saucepan. Simmer uncovered 5 minutes or until berries pop. Drain, then roll berries in sugar to coat.

Sugared Rosemary: Rinse fresh rosemary sprigs; pat dry. Brush leaves with warmed light corn syrup and immediately roll in granulated sugar. Store on a sugar-lined tray at room temperature.

Note: Spread hazelnuts in a baking pan. Bake at 350°F 8 to 10 minutes until toasted and papery skins begin to flake. Turn out onto a towel; rub off skins.

SERVES 8

PREP: 15 MIN   CHILL: AT LEAST 3 HR

- **1 qt fat-free half & half**
- **1 box (3.9 oz) instant chocolate pudding and pie filling (4-serving size)**
- **1 tsp ground cinnamon**
- **1 cup heavy (whipping) cream**
- **2 Tbsp sugar**
- **½ tsp vanilla extract**
- **Garnish: ground cinnamon**

FROZEN HOT CHOCOLATE

1. You'll need a 13 x 9-in. baking pan and eight glass 8-oz Irish coffee mugs or other 8-oz mugs.

2. Whisk half & half, pudding mix and cinnamon in a large bowl 2 minutes. Pour into baking pan; cover and freeze at least 3 hours, or until frozen hard.

3. About 20 minutes before serving: Beat cream, sugar and vanilla in a medium bowl with mixer on high speed until stiff peaks form when beaters are lifted. Refrigerate until ready to use.

4. Put coffee mugs in freezer. Remove mixture from freezer; leave at room temperature 15 minutes, or until it can be cut into large cubes. Place in food processor; pulse until smooth, scraping down sides occasionally. Divide among chilled mugs. Top with prepared whipped cream; sprinkle with cinnamon and serve.

Planning tip: Can be made through Step 2 up to two weeks ahead.

CHAPTER 4

SET THE MOOD

New Year's Eve and Valentine's Day are two holidays where food and beverages play a dual role: decor and menu. A beautiful spread, paired with the right music, creates a memorable celebration. To ring in the new year, add a little sparkle with silver and gold ribbon, tinsel and confetti. For Valentine's Day, lighting is key. Light up your night and fill every glass jar, vase and lamp with candles; cluster them all over the house. Dim the overhead lights and you're in business.

new year's *food*

CHAMPAGNE CHILLING

IN THE BUCKET SCREAMS

NEW YEAR'S EVE. TO

SHOWCASE YOUR FOOD,

USE CAREFULLY PLACED

TABLE STANDS.

SMOKY MARINATED SHRIMP

SERVES 12

PREP: 15 MIN   COOK: ABOUT 2 MIN
CHILL: OVERNIGHT

MARINADE

 1 **cup cider vinegar**

 1 **bottle (5 oz) chipotle hot
     pepper sauce (²/₃ cup)**

 ½ **cup ketchup**

 1 **Tbsp minced garlic**

 1 **tsp salt**

 1 **cup oil**

 2½ **lb large shrimp, peeled and
       deveined, tails left on**

 1   **each red and yellow pepper,
       cut in 1-in. pieces**

 1   **medium red onion,
       thinly sliced**

1. Marinade: Mix vinegar, hot pepper sauce, ketchup, garlic and salt in a large glass bowl. Whisk in oil until blended.

2. Add shrimp to a large saucepan of boiling water and cook 1 to 2 minutes until pink and just cooked through. Drain; chill under cold running water.

3. Add to Marinade along with the peppers and onion. Cover and refrigerate overnight.

4. To serve: Remove shrimp, peppers and onion with a slotted spoon to a serving bowl.

Planning tip: Best if prepared through Step 3 one day ahead.

MENU

• Smoky Marinated Shrimp

• Polenta Squares with
  Bolognese Topping

• Spanikopita Cups

• Roast Pork with
  Orange-Chili Sauce and
  Sicilian Slaw

• Petite Fruit Tarts

• Mini–Mochaccino Puddings

MAKES 70

PREP: 20 MIN   COOK: ABOUT 15 MIN
CHILL: 30 MIN

POLENTA

1 qt (4 cups) milk

½ tsp salt

¼ tsp pepper

1½ cups yellow cornmeal

½ cup each grated Parmesan
   and shredded fontina cheese

BOLOGNESE TOPPING

1 Tbsp olive oil

½ cup each chopped onion
   and shredded carrot

1 pkg (1¼ lb) Italian turkey sausage,
   removed from casings

1 can (14½ oz) petite-cut diced
   tomatoes with garlic and olive oil

Garnish: chopped parsley

MAKES 30

PREP: 20 MIN   COOK: 3 MIN   BAKE: 5 MIN

2 boxes (2.1 oz each) frozen mini
   fillo pastry shells (30 shells)

1 Tbsp olive oil

½ cup chopped scallions

1 tsp each minced garlic and
   chopped fresh dill

1 box (10 oz) frozen chopped
   spinach, thawed, not drained

¼ cup ⅓-less-fat cream cheese
   (Neufchâtel)

¼ tsp pepper

1 pkg (4 oz) crumbled feta cheese

2 Tbsp grated Parmesan

POLENTA SQUARES WITH BOLOGNESE TOPPING

1. Coat a 15½ x 10½-in. rimmed baking pan with nonstick spray.

2. Polenta: Heat milk, 1 cup water and the salt and pepper in a large saucepan over medium-high heat until simmering. Whisk in cornmeal and cook, whisking constantly, 3 minutes, or until thick and smooth. Remove from heat; stir in cheeses. Immediately pour into prepared pan; spread evenly. Cool; cover and refrigerate 30 minutes, or until firm.

3. Meanwhile, make **Topping:** Heat oil in a nonstick medium skillet over medium-high heat. Add onion and carrot; sauté 2 minutes until soft. Add turkey sausage; cook, breaking chunks into small pieces, 6 minutes, or until no longer pink. Add tomatoes and their juices; cook 1 minute to blend flavors.

4. To serve: Heat broiler. Line a baking sheet with foil. Cut polenta into 10 rows lengthwise, 7 rows crosswise. Place squares on prepared baking sheet. Broil 3 in. from heat source 5 to 6 minutes until polenta is browned.

5. Spoon 1 teaspoon warm topping on each square. Place on a serving platter.

Planning tip: Can be made through Step 3 up to one day ahead. Cover and refrigerate Polenta and Topping separately. Reheat Topping in microwave or on stovetop, then proceed as directed.

SPANIKOPITA CUPS

1. Heat oven to 400ºF. Place fillo shells on a rimmed baking sheet.

2. Heat oil in a nonstick medium skillet over medium heat. Add scallions, garlic and dill; cook 1 minute until soft. Add spinach and any liquid; cook 2 minutes until almost dry.

3. Add cream cheese and pepper; remove from heat and stir until cheese melts and mixture is blended.

4. Stir in feta and Parmesan cheese. Spoon 1 rounded measuring teaspoon into each shell.

5. To serve: Bake for 5 minutes, or until hot.

Planning tip: Can be made through Step 4 up to one day ahead. Cover and refrigerate.

ROAST PORK WITH ORANGE-CHILI SAUCE

SERVES 16

PREP: 20 MIN   COOK: 1 HR, PLUS 15 MIN
RESTING TIME   CHILL: OVERNIGHT

  1 **cup water**

  ¼ **cup each salt and sugar**

  1 **heaping Tbsp pickling spices**

  3 **cups apple juice or water**

4½ **lb pork loin roast**

  1 **Tbsp vegetable oil**

Tip: Brining the pork overnight with salt, sugar and spices ensures that the meat will be succulent—even if it roasts a bit longer than needed.

1. The day before making roast, boil 1 cup water in a 2-qt saucepan. Stir in the salt, sugar and pickling spices. Bring to boil and cook 1 minute or until sugar dissolves. Remove from heat. Cool 5 minutes.

2. Add apple juice to pickling liquid. Combine brine with pork in large ziptop bag wwor lidded container. Refrigerate overnight.

3. Heat oven to 375°F. Remove pork from brine, rinse and pat dry with paper towels. Rub oil over entire roast.

4. Heat a large skillet over medium-high heat. Place pork in pan and cook all sides until browned. Transfer to a roasting pan and cook for 55 to 60 minutes until temperature reaches 155°F. Remove from oven; cover with foil. Let rest 15 minutes.

ORANGE-CHILI SAUCE

Remove peel and white pith from 1 navel orange. Slice, then cut in bite-size pieces. In a bowl, whisk ½ cup pepper jelly until smooth. Stir in orange, 1 Tbsp chopped cilantro and 2 tsp minced jalapeño pepper. Makes about 1 cup.

SICILIAN SLAW

1. Whisk orange juice, oil, vinegar, sugar, salt and pepper in a large bowl until blended.

2. Add remaining ingredients except mint; toss to mix and coat. Cover and refrigerate at least 1 hour to blend flavors and slightly wilt cabbage.

3. When ready to serve, add mint and toss to mix.

SERVES 8

PREP: 15 MIN   CHILL: 1 HR

  ¾ **cup orange juice**

  6 **Tbsp olive oil**

  ⅓ **cup red wine vinegar**

1½ **Tbsp sugar**

  ½ **tsp each salt and pepper**

  4 **cups shredded savoy or regular green cabbage**

  2 **cups shredded red cabbage**

  1 **bulb fennel, trimmed, thinly sliced**

  ½ **cup each sliced red onion, pitted oil-cured olives and golden raisins**

  ½ **cup slivered fresh mint leaves**

PETITE FRUIT TARTS

1. Heat oven to 350°F. Line 2 baking sheets with foil. Placing a 4-in. plate or a 28-oz tomato can on the foil as a guide, use a toothpick to outline four 4-in. circles, about 1-in. apart, in each pan.

2. Crust: Put almonds, flour, granulated sugar and salt in food processor; pulse just until almonds are finely ground. Scatter butter over top; pulse until mixture resembles coarse crumbs. Add egg yolks and extract; pulse until dough clumps together. Remove blade; gather dough, place on wax paper and press into a 1-in.-thick disk. Cut, like a pie, in 8 wedges.

3. Place each wedge in an outlined circle; press to fill outline evenly. Crimp or press edges decoratively.

4. Bake 16 minutes or until edges are lightly browned. Slide foil with crusts (carefully, crusts are fragile) onto a wire rack to cool.

5. Meanwhile, grate 1 tsp zest and squeeze 2 Tbsp juice from the limes. Place in a large bowl with cream cheese and confectioners' sugar. Beat or whisk until smooth.

6. Shortly before serving, spread cream cheese mixture on crusts; top with cut-up fruit.

MAKES 8

PREP: 30 MIN   BAKE: ABOUT 26 MIN
COOL (CRUSTS): 10 MIN

CRUST

- ⅔ **cup slivered almonds, toasted** *(see Note)*
- 1½ **cups all-purpose flour**
- ¼ **cup granulated sugar**
- ½ **tsp salt**
- ⅔ **cup (1 stick plus 2 Tbsp and 2 tsp) cold butter, cut in small pieces**
- 2 **large egg yolks**
- ½ **tsp almond extract**

- 2 **limes**
- 1 **brick (8 oz) cream cheese, softened**
- ½ **cup confectioners' sugar**
- 3 **cups cut-up fruit (we used kiwi, pineapple, strawberries and oranges)**

Note: To toast almonds, spread them in a baking pan or on a microwave-safe plate. Stirring a few times, bake in 350°F oven 8 to 10 minutes or microwave on high about 4 minutes until fragrant and lightly browned. Cool completely.

Planning tip: The crusts can be baked and cream cheese mixture made up to one week ahead. Store crusts airtight at room temperature; refrigerate cheese mixture. Cut fruits and mix up to 2 hours before serving. Refrigerate covered.

MAKES 12

PREP: 10 MIN   CHILL: 1 HR

  4 **cups milk**

 ⅔ **cup sugar**

 ¼ **cup cornstarch**

  2 **Tbsp unsweetened cocoa**

  1 **Tbsp instant espresso powder**

 ⅛ **tsp salt**

  8 **oz bittersweet chocolate, broken up**

  1 **Tbsp vanilla extract**

  1 **cup heavy cream**

  2 **Tbsp confectioners' sugar**

Garnish: ground cinnamon

MINI–MOCHACCINO PUDDINGS

1. Whisk milk, sugar, cornstarch, cocoa, espresso powder and salt in a large saucepan until blended. Bring to a boil over medium-high heat, stirring often with a whisk and making sure to reach into corners of saucepan.

2. Boil 1 minute, whisking, until thickened. Remove from heat; stir in chocolate and vanilla until chocolate is melted and mixture is smooth.

3. Pour into twelve 3- to 4-oz espresso or other small cups or glasses. Cover with wax paper; refrigerate at least 1 hour or until firm.

4. To serve: Beat cream and confectioners' sugar until very soft peaks form. Spread over tops of pudding. Stir ground cinnamon through a strainer to garnish.

valentine's *decor*

CELEBRATE THE DAY OF
AMOUR WITH LITTLE
GESTURES—POUR YOUR
HEART OUT AND GIVE
SMALL SURPRISES THAT
SAY I LOVE YOU

2

1. Flower power

According to a recent study, people who made a point of looking at flowers first thing in the morning reported feeling cheerier and even more energetic throughout the day. That goes double on Valentine's Day!

2. Valentine's bookmark

A favorite Valentine's Day card can hold a place in your heart—and in the book you're reading. Every time you open the pages, the bookmark is a sweet reminder of those who love and cherish you.

3. Let it snow!

To make, cut a circle of oven-bake clay to fit in the lid of a screw-top jar. Press an indent in the center; bake clay at 275°F for 15 minutes. Super-Glue clay to inside of lid. Glue a heart bead in the indent (or thread a thin wire through a bead with a hole and insert, as we did here). Add ½ tsp glitter to the jar, fill with water, then screw on lid.

4

4. Romantic scents

Extend the life of your Valentine's Day blooms. Dry out the petals and mix with your favorite blend of herbs, spices and cinnamon sticks.

Be creative

Give your loved ones chocolate, but don't forget to deliver the drama with a homemade gift that shows how much you adore them.

valentine's
food

SERVE A RED-HOT MENU
IN VARIOUS HUES OF
RED TO RATCHET UP
THE ROMANCE. YOUR
SWEETHEART WILL HAVE
TO SUCCUMB!

TUSCAN TOMATO SOUP

SERVES 4

PREP: 5 MIN   COOK: 10 MIN

 1 **jar (24 to 26 oz) marinara sauce**

 1 **can (19 oz) cannellini beans, rinsed**

 1 **jar (7 oz) roasted red peppers**

 2 **Tbsp extra-virgin olive oil**

 1 **clove garlic**

1¾ **cups chicken broth**

 ¼ **cup thin strips fresh basil leaves**

   Freshly ground pepper, to taste

Serve with: Parmesan Toasts
(recipe follows)

1. Put sauce, beans, peppers, oil and garlic in a blender or food processor; process until smooth. Pour into a medium saucepan along with the broth. Stirring often, bring to a simmer over medium-high heat.

2. Remove from heat; stir in basil. Spoon into bowls; grind pepper on top.

PARMESAN TOASTS

Heat broiler. Line a baking sheet with foil. Place 12 thin slices French bread on foil; sprinkle each slice with 1 tsp grated Parmesan cheese. Broil 2 to 3 minutes until lightly toasted.

Simply romantic

The most important aspect of this day is not price, but thoughtfulness. Create a fabulous candlelit dinner for your loved one. Scatter a rose-petal path leading to the table laden with your beloved's favorite foods (certain to win him or her over and have an aphrodisiac effect).

CHICKEN WITH RUBY GRAPEFRUIT & CRANBERRY SALSA

1. Mix flour, paprika and salt in a plastic food bag. Add chicken; shake to coat.

2. Heat oil in a large nonstick skillet. Add chicken and cook, turning once, 6 to 8 minutes until browned and cooked through.

3. Meanwhile, mix Salsa ingredients in a bowl to blend. Serve with chicken.

SERVES 4

PREP: 10 MIN   COOK: ABOUT 8 MIN

- 2   **Tbsp flour**
- 1   **tsp paprika**
- ½   **tsp salt**
- 4   **skinless, boneless chicken breast halves (about 6 oz each)**
- 2   **tsp oil**

SALSA

- 1   **can (16 oz) whole-berry cranberry sauce**
- 1   **large ruby grapefruit, peeled and white pith removed, cut in sections, sections halved (or 1 cup bottled red grapefruit sections, sections halved)**
- 2   **Tbsp each sliced scallions and fresh mint**
- 1   **Tbsp minced, seeded red jalapeño pepper**
- 1   **Tbsp chopped crystallized ginger**

SERVES 6

PREP: 10 MIN   COOK: ABOUT 30 MIN

1½ **lb lean ground beef**

 1 **large red onion, chopped**

 1 **medium red pepper, chopped**

 3 **Tbsp chili powder**

 2 **tsp minced garlic**

 2 **tsp cumin seeds or
     ground cumin**

 1 **tsp dried oregano**

½ **tsp salt**

 1 **can (28 oz) fire-roasted
     crushed tomatoes**

 1 **can (15 oz) red kidney
     beans, rinsed**

 1 **cup water**

 1 **Tbsp chopped bittersweet
     chocolate (optional)**

**Toppings: shredded Cheddar,
    chopped red onion, red
    pepper and cilantro**

**Garnish: sliced avocado and red
    pepper (optional)**

BOWL OF RED

1. Heat a large, deep nonstick skillet over medium-high heat. Add beef, onion and red pepper. Cook 5 minutes, stirring to break up meat, until it is no longer pink.

2. Stir in chili powder, garlic, cumin, oregano and salt. Cook, stirring, 1 minute or until fragrant. Stir in tomatoes, beans and water; bring to a boil. Reduce heat, cover and simmer 15 minutes to develop flavors.

3. Remove from heat; stir in chocolate (if using) until melted. Serve with some or all of the toppings.

FROZEN BERRY ANGEL SHORTCAKE

1. Prepare the Classic Angel Food Cake *(recipe below)*, with these changes: Line the bottom of a 9 x 3-in. springform pan with nonstick foil, then attach the sides of the pan. Substitute **raspberry extract** for the vanilla in Step 3, and add **3 drops liquid red food color** with the extract. Spread in prepared pan and bake as directed. Cool the cake completely, in pan, upside down on a wire rack. To loosen cake, run a thin-bladed knife around sides of pan; remove pan sides. Invert cake and remove pan bottom.

2. To assemble Shortcake: Using a serrated knife, cut cake into 2 layers. Place bottom layer, cut side up, on pan bottom and spread with **⅓ cup strawberry topping**. Spoon **3 cups slightly softened lowfat strawberry ice cream or frozen yogurt** over topping. Spread **another ⅓ cup strawberry topping** over ice cream. Top with remaining cake layer, cut side down. Freeze at least 4 hours or overnight. (Once the cake is frozen, it can be wrapped and stored in freezer up to 2 weeks.)

3. To serve: Transfer frozen cake to a serving plate. Frost with **2 cups thawed lite whipped topping or lightly sweetened whipped cream**. Decorate with **strawberries or raspberries**. Refrigerate 30 minutes to soften slightly before serving.

SERVES 12

PREP: 30 MIN   BAKE: 35 MIN
FREEZE: AT LEAST 4 HR

- 1 cup cake flour (not self-rising)
- 1¼ cups granulated sugar
- ¼ tsp salt
- 10 large egg whites (1⅓ to 1½ cups), at room temperature
- 1 tsp cream of tartar
- 2 tsp vanilla extract

CLASSIC ANGEL FOOD CAKE

1. Adjust oven rack to lowest position; heat oven to 350°F. You'll need a 10-in. tube pan with removable bottom. Line bottom with nonstick foil, cutting to fit around the tube; place back into pan.

2. Whisk together cake flour, ¼ cup sugar and the salt; transfer mixture to a sieve set over a small bowl.

3. In large bowl, beat the egg whites with electric mixer on medium speed 2 minutes until frothy and well blended. Add the cream of tartar; increase speed to medium-high and beat until soft peaks start to form, about 3 minutes. While still beating, add the remaining 1 cup sugar in a slow stream; continue to beat until whites are very thick and hold firm peaks when beaters are lifted, about 3 minutes. Beat in the vanilla.

4. Transfer mixture to a large, wide bowl. Sift ⅓ of the flour mixture over whites; fold in with a rubber spatula. Repeat twice with the remaining flour, folding in until incorporated. Scrape batter into pan and spread evenly. Run a knife through the batter to remove any air pockets.

5. Bake 35 minutes, or until top of cake springs back when pressed with fingertip or a skewer inserted into cake comes out clean. Immediately invert the pan onto a wire rack. Cool completely, upside down.

6. To loosen cake, run a knife around all sides of pan. Lift cake out of pan by tube. Loosen cake from bottom; invert to unmold.

VALENTINE COOKIE BOUQUETS

1. Beat butter and sugars in large bowl with mixer until light and fluffy, about 3 minutes. Beat in egg until blended; add vanilla, baking powder, cardamom and salt. Gradually add flour and beat until just smooth. Shape dough into a disk; cover with plastic wrap and refrigerate 1 hour.

2. Heat oven to 350°F. Line 2 baking sheets with parchment paper or nonstick foil. Roll out dough between 2 sheets parchment or wax paper to ³⁄₈-in. thickness. Cut out 8 hearts with cookie cutter. Transfer 4 hearts to each prepared baking sheet with small spatula. Insert the point of a skewer (by gently twirling it between your thumb and index finger) about 2½ in. into dough through pointed tip of each heart. Gather and refrigerate dough scraps.

3. Bake 12 to 14 minutes, until cookies are golden brown at edges. Cool on sheet on wire rack 5 minutes; transfer to rack and cool completely. Roll, cut and bake remaining hearts as directed above.

4. Divide decorating icing into 3 bowls. Tint one bowl red and one pink; leave one white. Transfer half of each color batch to separate pastry bags fitted with plain writing tips; refrigerate pastry bags. Thin the remaining icing with a few tsp water to the consistency of slightly whipped cream. Spread thinned icing over hearts; let dry completely. Outline hearts and decorate with patterns using the thick icing in pastry bags. Let designs dry completely.

MAKES 14 COOKIES

PREP: 30 MIN   CHILL: 1 HR
BAKE: 12–14 MIN PER BATCH

- **1   stick (½ cup) unsalted butter, softened**
- **⅓   cup granulated sugar**
- **¼   cup packed light brown sugar**
- **1   large egg**
- **1½ tsp vanilla extract**
- **½   tsp baking powder**
- **½   tsp ground cardamom (optional)**
- **¼   tsp salt**
- **1¾ cups all-purpose flour**
- **Decorating Icing** *(recipe below)*

You'll also need: 3-in. heart-shaped cookie cutter; 15 (10-in.) bamboo skewers; red gel food color; 3 pastry bags with plain writing tips; tall glasses or vases; plastic foam (Styrofoam); granulated sugar

Decorating Icing: Beat 1 lb confectioners' sugar and ½ cup powdered egg whites, found in your store's baking section, in large bowl with mixer on low speed to blend. Beat in ⅓ cup water. Increase speed to high; beat 5 minutes or until icing is very thick and white. Makes 2½ cups.

To assemble: Fill glasses or vases with foam blocks cut to fit. Pour in sugar between glass and foam to cover. Trim skewers to varying lengths and insert into foam (space the cookies evenly so they're balanced to prevent tipping).

Planning tip: You can bake and decorate cookies up to 4 days ahead. Store covered at room temperature.

PEACH MELBA CUPCAKES

1. Prepare the Classic Angel Food Cake
(recipe on page 95), with these changes: You'll
need 24 jumbo paper cupcake liners. Double
up the liners, 2 per cupcake, and arrange on a large
baking sheet. After adding flour in Step 4, spoon
the batter into a gallon-size ziptop bag; seal
bag and cut off a ½-in. corner. Pipe the batter
into the liners, filling each almost to the top. Smooth
tops with an offset spatula. Bake 20 minutes, or
until pick inserted in centers comes out clean. Cool
on baking sheet on wire rack.

2. Melba Sauce: Purée in a blender **1 thawed
10-oz package frozen raspberries in syrup**.
Scrape berry mixture through a fine-mesh sieve set
over medium bowl to remove seeds; discard seeds.

3. To assemble Cupcakes: You'll need **1 thawed
1-lb bag frozen sliced peaches** (any thick slices
should be cut into thinner slices). If desired, toss
peaches with **¼ cup sugar**. Carefully peel back
inner paper liner; remove cupcake. Slice off rounded
top with a serrated knife; cut top into quarters.
Place cupcake bottom back into outer paper liner
and spoon some Melba Sauce over cut surface. Top
with a dollop of **whipped nondairy topping**. Place
3 or 4 peach slices into whipped topping. Drizzle
with more sauce; add another dollop of whipped
topping. Stick cupcake-top quarters into cream.

HERE IS AN EGG-CELLENT
ALTERNATIVE TO
TRADITIONAL EASTER
EGG DECORATING.
PAINT HARD-BOILED
OR BLOWN EGGS
YOURSELF WITH BLACK
CHALKBOARD PAINT
(SPRAY OR BRUSH-ON),
THEN LET KIDS GO
TO TOWN WITH
COLORED CHALK.

CHAPTER 5

GLORIOUS
SPRINGTIME
ENTERTAINING

Spring is in the air, which means Easter is right around the corner. With warmer weather calling, it's time to plan an homage to the festival of hope and renewal. And what could be more joyous than celebrating with family and friends? Effortless entertaining is a breeze when you spring into action and plan a simple and delicious menu ahead of time. You'll even have energy left over to hunt for eggs!

THIS EASTER HOLIDAY,

DINE ON EASY

TRADITIONAL DISHES

AND WHIMSICAL

DESSERTS, MADE WITH

BRIGHT SPRING PRODUCE

APRICOT-GLAZED SMOKED HAM

SERVES 8 (WITH LEFTOVERS)

PREP: 10 MIN   BAKE: 2½ HR
REST: 20 MIN

- **1   ready-to-cook bone-in smoked ham half (8 to 10 lb), preferably shank end**

Whole cloves

- **3   cups water**

GLAZE

- **1   jar (12-oz) apricot preserves (1 cup)**
- **¼   cup light brown sugar**
- **2   Tbsp grainy Dijon mustard (we used Maille)**
- **1   Tbsp cider vinegar**

1. Position oven rack in bottom third of oven; heat to 325°F. You'll need a shallow roasting pan.

2. Cut off thick rind on ham to expose the fat layer underneath, leaving about 5 inches of the rind intact covering the narrow shank end. Using a sharp knife, score fat in diamond pattern. Press 1 clove into center of each diamond. Place ham in roasting pan; pour water in pan. Cover loosely with heavy-duty foil. Roast ham 1½ hours.

3. Meanwhile, mix Glaze ingredients. Remove ham from oven; brush with one-third of the glaze. Continue to bake, uncovered, 1 hour, brushing with remaining glaze every 20 minutes, or until internal temperature registers 160°F on an instant-read thermometer.

4. Let ham rest 20 minutes. Transfer to platter. Serve ham hot, warm, or at room temperature.

Planning tip: Let ham come to room temperature, covered, about 2 hours before baking.

MENU

- Apricot-Glazed Smoked Ham
- Warm Potato Salad Dijonnaise
- Sweet Spiced Baby Carrots
- Double Berry Tarts
- Coconut Chiffon Cake
- Spring Cupcakes

SERVES 8

PREP: 15 MIN   COOK: 12–15 MIN

1½ **lb each baby red and Yukon Gold potatoes, halved (quartered if larger)**

3 **Tbsp creamy Dijon mustard**

2 **Tbsp each seasoned rice vinegar and olive oil**

1 **Tbsp fresh tarragon, chopped**

1½ **tsp kosher salt**

½ **tsp freshly ground pepper**

4 **scallions, thinly sliced**

WARM POTATO SALAD DIJONNAISE

1. Place potatoes in a large pot and fill with cold water to cover by 1 in. Bring to a boil, reduce heat to medium, and gently boil 12 to 15 minutes, until potatoes are just tender when pierced with tip of a knife. Drain in colander.

2. In large bowl, whisk mustard, vinegar, olive oil, tarragon, salt and pepper. Add potatoes and scallions; gently toss until evenly coated. Serve immediately while still warm or at room temperature.

Planning tip: You can boil potatoes 1 day ahead, cool, cover and refrigerate. Reheat in the microwave just before tossing with the dressing.

SERVES 6

PREP: 5 MIN   COOK: ABOUT 20 MIN

  2 **Tbsp olive oil**

1½ **lb whole baby carrots (peeled and trimmed if with stems), halved lengthwise if thick**

  1 **tsp ground cumin**

  ½ **cup each orange juice and water**

  2 **Tbsp sugar**

  ¼ **tsp each salt and freshly ground pepper**

Planning tip: You can purchase baby carrots with stems and greens or just buy the bags of prepeeled. Prepare a day ahead and refrigerate.

SWEET SPICED BABY CARROTS

1. Heat oil over medium-high heat in large nonstick skillet. Add carrots and cumin; cook 2 minutes.

2. Add remaining ingredients. Simmer, uncovered, on medium-low 20 minutes or until carrots are fork-tender.

DOUBLE BERRY TARTS

SERVES 8

PREP: 30 MIN   FREEZE: 1 HR
BAKE: 24 MIN

¼   **cup each sliced almonds and granulated sugar**

1   **pkg (17.3-oz) frozen puff pastry sheets (2 sheets), thawed**

1   **large egg white, lightly beaten**

8   **large strawberries, hulled**

2   **containers (6 oz each) raspberries**

Garnish: confectioners' sugar

1. Pulse almonds and granulated sugar in food processor until nuts are finely ground (store at room temperature in a ziptop bag up to 2 weeks before using).

2. You'll need a baking sheet lined with wax or parchment paper. Unfold one pastry sheet on a lightly floured surface; gently roll out seams with rolling pin until surface is flat. Cut into four 5-in. squares.

3. Working with one pastry square at a time, cut off a ½-in.-wide strip from each side of the square. Brush edges of square with egg white; top each side of the square with a dough strip, building a double-thick pastry edge. Square off edges of tarts with a large knife. Crimp pastry edges with a fork.

4. Transfer tart shells to prepared baking sheet. Repeat with remaining pastry, making a total of 8 tart shells. Freeze shells 1 hour or until hard; transfer to a freezer container lined with wax paper, or bake and serve.

5. When ready to bake, heat oven to 400°F. You'll need a large baking sheet lined with nonstick foil. Remove frozen tart shells and sprinkle surface of each shell (including edges) with a rounded tsp almond sugar; place on prepared baking sheet. Cut a strawberry in 4 slices and overlap in center of each tart shell. Sprinkle with ½ tsp almond sugar. Bake 24 minutes, or until puffed and golden.

6. Cool tarts on sheet on wire rack 10 minutes. Top tarts with fresh raspberries. Serve warm or at room temperature, dusted with confectioners' sugar.

Planning tip: You can make and freeze unfilled tart shells up to 3 weeks before baking. Fill unthawed shells and bake right before serving.

SERVES 12

PREP: 15 MIN   BAKE: 1 HR

CAKE

- 6 **large egg whites, at room temperature**
- ¼ **tsp cream of tartar**
- ¼ **cup sugar**
- 1 **box (18.25-oz) white cake mix**
- 1 **can (14-oz) lite unsweetened coconut milk**
- 1 **Tbsp oil**
- 2 **tsp coconut extract**
- 18 **drops liquid yellow food color**

COCONUT FROSTING

- ¾ **cup each cream cheese frosting (from a 12-oz tub) and marshmallow creme (Fluff)**
- 1½ **cups sweetened flaked coconut**

Planning tip: You can bake and frost cake up to 2 days before serving. Store, covered, at room temperature.

COCONUT CHIFFON CAKE

1. Heat oven to 325°F. You'll need a 10-inch tube pan with removable core and bottom (not nonstick).

2. Cake: Beat egg whites and cream of tartar in large bowl with mixer on medium until soft peaks form when beaters are lifted. Gradually beat in sugar until incorporated. Continue to beat on high until stiff, shiny peaks form.

3. In a second large bowl (no need to wash beaters), beat remaining cake ingredients on medium speed until blended. Continue to beat on high until smooth, about 3 minutes. Add egg whites to top of batter and fold in with rubber spatula until combined. Scrape batter into ungreased pan; smooth top and tap pan on counter a few times to settle batter.

4. Bake 1 hour or until toothpick inserted in center comes out clean. Invert pan onto its core on countertop and cool cake completely.

5. Loosen cake around sides of pan and core with long thin-bladed knife; lift cake from pan sides by the tube. Cut away cake from pan bottom and invert onto a rack, then immediately reinvert cake right side up on a serving plate.

6. Coconut Frosting: Fold cream cheese frosting and marshmallow creme together in a medium bowl until blended. Spread evenly over cake. Cover frosting with coconut, gently pressing to adhere.

MORPHOS BUTTERFLIES

1. Pairs of wings and antennae: Draw templates for wings and antennae freehand, then place them on baking sheets; cover with wax paper.

2. Put 1 cup each dark cocoa and blue candy melting wafers into separate ziptop bags; do not seal. Microwave 10 seconds to soften. Squeeze, return to microwave and repeat until smooth. Press out excess air and seal.

3. Snip a tiny corner from each bag. Working on one wing at a time, use melted dark cocoa to outline template on wax paper. Go over outline to thicken. Fill in with melted blue candy. Then, following the shape of the wing's outer edge, pipe a line of dark cocoa on the blue portion of the upper and lower wings. Tap the pan slightly to flatten. With toothpick, pull dark cocoa into blue to make the design.

4. While candy is still liquid, sprinkle top and bottom wing tips with yellow nonpareils. Repeat, melting additional wafers several seconds in the microwave as needed (be careful not to overheat). Chill baking sheets until set, about 5 minutes. Repeat for antennae, using melted dark cocoa.

5. Spoon chocolate frosting into a ziptop bag, press out excess air, seal and set aside. Spread vanilla frosting on top of cupcakes; roll edges in white decorating sugar.

6. Carefully peel chilled wings and antennae from wax paper. Place 2 brown M&M's, ½ in. apart, on top of cupcakes to support wings. Press inside edge of a pair of wings into frosting about ¼ in. apart, leaning wings on M&M's. Gently press antennae into frosting at head of butterfly. For body, snip a small corner from the bag with chocolate frosting. Starting at antennae, pipe 4 or 5 beads of frosting down the length of body, drawing frosting into a small point on the last bead.

MAKES 12 CUPCAKES

TIME: DEPENDS ON DECORATING SKILLS

- 1½ **cups dark cocoa melting wafers**
- 1½ **cups blue candy melting wafers**
- 2 **Tbsp yellow nonpareils**
- ¾ **cup dark chocolate frosting**
- 1½ **cups vanilla frosting**
- 12 **vanilla cupcakes baked in white paper liners**
- ¾ **cup white coarse decorating sugar**
- 24 **brown M&M's**

Planning tip: You can make wings and antennae up to 2 days ahead; store loosely covered at cool room temperature.

DAISIES, PHLOX AND BEES

1. Daisies: Draw a flower petal template freehand, then place it on a baking sheet and cover with wax paper. Put white chocolate melting wafers in a ziptop bag; do not seal. Microwave 10 seconds to soften. Squeeze, return to microwave and repeat until smooth. Press out excess air and seal. Snip a small corner from the bag. Pipe outline of the petal with melted chocolate and fill in with more chocolate. Tap pan lightly to settle. Repeat, making 108 petals. Refrigerate to set, about 5 minutes.

2. Phlox: Sprinkle work surface with the orange sugar. Press 2 orange spice drops together and roll out on the sugared surface to 1/16 in. thick. Draw your own templates freehand, cut out the flower shapes with clean scissors. Repeat with the remaining sugar and the spice drops of each color to make about 30 flowers.

3. Bees: For each bee, cut a licorice lace into three ¾-in. pieces; cut each in half lengthwise for antennae. Cut 3 pieces of licorice into ½-in. pieces and taper one end for the stinger.

4. Cut the blackberry candy in half crosswise. Place a yellow M&M flat against the cut side of a blackberry candy piece. Place the other cut end on the other side of the M&M, to sandwich. Trim a small slice from flat end of the blackberry candy. Attach 2 pieces of licorice as antennae, and another M&M as the head.

5. Spoon ¼ cup vanilla frosting into a ziptop bag, press out excess air and seal. Spread remaining vanilla frosting on top of cupcakes.

6. Peel white chocolate petals from wax paper. Cut orange spice drops in half crosswise. Using about 6 petals per flower, arrange 3 flowers on each of six cupcakes. Place orange spice drops, cut side down, in center of petals. Add spearmint leaf slices.

7. Using 5 flowers per cupcake, arrange phlox on cupcakes. Pipe a small dot of white frosting in the center of each flower and add a sunflower seed. Add spearmint leaves.

8. Put 2 bee bodies on top of a cupcake. Add licorice stingers at tail ends. Press 2 almond slices into frosting as wings.

Planning tip: You can make and decorate up to 2 days ahead. Cover; store at cool room temperature.

Note: Chocolate-covered sunflower seeds can be found at Trader Joe's and the Sweet Factory at most malls, as well as online.

MAKES 12 CUPCAKES

TIME: DEPENDS ON DECORATING SKILLS

- 1½ **cups white chocolate melting wafers**
- ¼ **cup each orange, pink and yellow decorating sugar**
- 50 **assorted orange, pink and yellow spice drops**
- **Black licorice laces**
- 24 **blackberry jellies with black nonpareils, or Crows or black gumdrops**
- 48 **yellow M&M's**
- 1 **can (16 oz) vanilla frosting**
- 12 **vanilla cupcakes baked in white paper liners**
- **Multicolored chocolate-covered sunflower seeds (see Note)**
- 24 **candy spearmint leaves, sliced horizontally in thirds**
- 48 **natural almond slices**

4TH OF JULY
AND SUMMER
PARTIES

Summertime, and the livin' is easy.... It's also time to have friends and family over to enjoy those warm sunny days and evenings together. Whatever the occasion, dining al fresco and enjoying summer's bounty is one of life's simplest pleasures. It doesn't cost a fortune, either! Plan a barbecue or cool cocktails on the patio, or try a poolside brunch or festive south-of-the border Fourth of July fête. Make sure to dress up your backyard with colorful accents to fit the theme.

SUMMER PARTIES | 109

summer fun
crafts

PEOPLE LOVE A

CASUAL GET-TOGETHER,

SO FORGO THE TYPICAL

SIT-DOWN DINNER AND

GO FOR A GATHERING

OUT ON THE DECK

1. The great outdoors

Pay the same attention to your outdoor decor as you do inside. Simple touches like colorful textiles and a framed menu will make guests feel special.

2. Name game

Place-card napkin tags add a personal touch. Cut the tag from festive paper, hole-punch the top and tie to your favorite napkin rings with a ribbon.

3. Going green

Recycle old tin cans into stylish utensil holders or flower vases. You'll need about 2½ yards of velvet ribbon, ¾ to 1½ inches wide, to decorate each can. Using a hot-glue gun, place a dab of glue on the top side of the can. Wind the ribbon downward around the can, overlapping each layer about ¼ inch, making sure there aren't any gaps and dabbing more glue along the way. At the bottom, trim the ribbon and affix with a final dab of glue.

Details, details

Dig out fun fabrics and paper you've been waiting to use, and put them to work. Cover ordinary objects and make them extraordinary.

SERVE CROWD-PLEASING RECIPES THAT ALLOW YOU TO ENJOY THE FESTIVITIES. A HELP-YOURSELF MEXICAN BUFFET DOES THE TRICK.

SLOW-COOKER DIY FESTIVE FAJITAS

SERVES 8

PREP: 10 MIN   COOK: 8–10 HR (LOW)

- 1 **cup Mexican-style fajita sauce and marinade**
- 1 **Tbsp chopped garlic**
- 3 **lb boneless pork shoulder, well trimmed**
- 2 **medium red peppers, cut in ½-in.-wide strips**
- 1 **medium red onion, thinly sliced**
- ¼ **cup fresh lime juice**
- ¼ **tsp salt**
- ½ **cup chopped fresh cilantro**

Serve with: soft flour tortillas, assorted taco shells, guacamole, shredded lettuce and salsa

1. Mix fajita sauce and garlic in 4-qt or larger slow-cooker. Add pork; turn to coat. Scatter peppers around pork. Cover and cook on low 8 to 10 hours until pork is very tender.

2. At least 20 minutes or up to 2 hours before serving, toss onion slices with lime juice and salt in a small serving bowl. Then refrigerate, tossing occasionally, until onions are slightly wilted.

3. Remove pork to a cutting board. Shred with 2 forks into bite-size pieces. Return to slow-cooker; stir in cilantro.

4. Spoon into a serving bowl and let guests fill their own tortillas or taco shells. Serve with the onions, guacamole, shredded lettuce and salsa.

Beat the heat

Think the slow-cooker is only for winter? Think again! When you throw a slow-cooker summer soirée, your kitchen stays cool in the warm weather, a major bonus, not to mention the one-pot convenience. You can create tasty, appealing, simple suppers that sizzle, even when you're not using the grill.

WATERMELON FETA SALAD WITH MINT AND HONEY CITRUS DRIZZLE

Arrange the watermelon cubes in six individual salad bowls and sprinkle with feta cheese. In a separate bowl, whisk together the honey, poppy seeds and lemon juice. Drizzle over the watermelon salads and garnish each with fresh mint.

Planning tip: Sweet watermelon combines with salty feta and fresh mint for a vibrant fruit salad that is a must-have for brunch. The Honey Citrus Drizzle is super-simple and can be made a day in advance.

SERVES 6

PREP: 15 MIN   ASSEMBLE: 10 MIN

SALAD

- 6 cups watermelon, cut into ½-inch cubes
- 6 oz feta cheese, crumbled
- 2 Tbsp fresh mint, shredded

HONEY CITRUS DRIZZLE

- 4 Tbsp honey
- 1 tsp poppy seeds
- Juice of 4 lemons

TOMATO-BAKED EGGS

Heat oven to 400°F. Place tomatoes in a buttered baking dish and season generously with salt, pepper and parsley. Break one egg in each tomato and bake for 20 minutes or until egg is cooked to your liking. Garnish with shredded basil and Parmesan cheese.

Note: The bright red color of this delicious dish makes it a standout centerpiece on any brunch table. Assemble it a few hours in advance, then stick it in the refrigerator.

SERVES 6

PREP: 15 MIN   BAKE: 20 MIN

- Butter
- 6 beefsteak tomatoes, ripe but firm, hollowed out
- Salt and pepper, to taste
- 6 tsp chopped flat-leaf parsley
- 6 eggs
- 1 Tbsp fresh basil, shredded
- Parmesan cheese, shaved

CRÊPE-STYLE PANCAKES WITH PECAN PRALINES

SERVES 6

PREP: 10 MIN   COOK: ABOUT 35 MIN

PRALINES

1   cup dark maple syrup

¾   cup pecans, roughly chopped

CRÊPES

Zest of 1 orange

2   Tbsp butter, room temperature

1   cup all-purpose flour

2   large eggs

¼   cup water

½   cup milk

¼   cup orange juice

Pinch of salt

Vegetable oil

1½   cups dark maple syrup

5   oz crème fraîche

1. Pralines: In a medium saucepan, bring maple syrup to a boil; add pecans. Stir occasionally for about 10 minutes, remove from heat and stir for a few minutes. Mixture should be thick; if not, return saucepan to heat and stir constantly for a few more minutes. Pour mixture onto a foil-lined baking sheet to cool. When hardened, crumble and set aside.

2. In a small bowl, mix together orange zest and butter. Set aside.

3. With an electric mixer, combine flour and eggs on low speed. Slowly add water, milk and orange juice, and mix until smooth. Add orange zest–butter mixture and salt; mix until combined. Batter should be very thin. If too thick, add a bit more milk.

4. In a large skillet over medium heat add 2 tsp vegetable oil. When the skillet is hot but not smoking, pour in ½ to ⅓ cup batter and gently move it around the pan with a spoon until you have a very thin, wide pancake, about 8 inches in diameter. Cook each side about 1 minute, or until golden. Stack on a paper towel–lined plate and keep warm in the oven until the batch is finished. Roll up and garnish with maple syrup, pralines and crème fraîche.

MAKES 22 CUPS

PREP: 30 MIN   CHILL: AT LEAST 1 HR

- 3 bottles (750 ml each) dry white wine *(see Note)*
- ½ cup triple sec or other orange liqueur
- 1½ cups no-pulp orange juice
- ¼ cup fresh lemon juice
- 6 Tbsp sugar, or to taste
- 4 ripe peaches, cut in thin wedges
- 2 pt (12 oz each) strawberries, sliced
- 1 each lemon, lime and orange, cut in thin half-slices
- 1 Golden Delicious apple, cut in thin wedges
- 2 trays ice cubes

WHITE SANGRIA

1. Stir first 5 ingredients in a large bowl until sugar dissolves. Refrigerate to chill.

2. One hour before serving, pour mixture into pitcher(s); add fruit. Refrigerate.

3. To serve, add ice to pitchers.

Note: For a nonalcoholic version, use 9 cups 100% white grape juice in place of wine, omit triple sec and sugar, and increase orange juice to 2 cups.

Planning tip: Can be prepared through Step 1 up to one day ahead. Start cutting fruit about 1 hour and 15 minutes before serving.

CHAPTER 7

SPECIAL
OCCASIONS

When the holidays are over or you just need an excuse to entertain, it's good to have a few tricks up your sleeve to host an inexpensive theme party or a casual family gathering. Special occasions abound, whether it's birthdays and anniversaries, graduations and reunions, or even good old-fashioned poker night. Here are the basic rules: Invite the guests, plan the menu, organize the activities, create some decorations to personalize it, and most important, have a blast!

special occasions
crafts

DRESS UP A PLAIN GLASS

OBJECT WITH THE EASY

TECHNIQUE OF ETCHING.

THESE IDEAS SUIT EVERY

SKILL LEVEL AND CREATE

CONVERSATION PIECES

3. Cake dome creation

A pretty paisley pattern turns an ordinary Cake Dome* into a glamorous serving piece fit for royalty.

1. Great glasses

Turn mismatched Drinking Glasses* into a cohesive set with a fun design you make yourself. Use tape strips for a striped effect, or round stickers for whimsical dots.

2. Pitcher with pizzazz

Turn an old pitcher into a brand-new juice container. Tape your pattern inside, making it straight. Then adhere shelving paper to the outside of the Pitcher.* Use a craft knife to make each cutout. Peel off and apply etching cream as instructed.

Special effects

Timing and neatness are important skills to have when attempting to etch on glass. Start with simple shapes until you get the technique down.

* For instructions, see p. 143.

special occasions
food

MAKE SURE THE MENU
FITS THE OCCASION,
WHETHER IT'S AN
ANNIVERSARY, BIRTHDAY
OR A GATHERING OF
FAMILY OR FRIENDS

HEARTY SAUSAGE, SQUASH & BEAN SOUP

SERVES 12

PREP: 20 MIN   COOK: ABOUT 1 HR 15 MIN

1   lb sweet or hot Italian
    sausage, casings removed

1   large onion, chopped

4   medium carrots, sliced

3   celery stalks, sliced

3   large garlic cloves, crushed
    through a press

3   cans (15 to 19 oz each)
    cannellini beans, rinsed
    and drained

1   can (14 oz) chicken broth

4   cups water

1   can (14.5 oz) fire-roasted
    diced tomatoes

1   medium butternut squash,
    peeled, seeded, and cut
    into ½-in. chunks

1   head escarole, cut into shreds

¾   tsp salt

Freshly ground black pepper
    to taste

1. Spray a 6- to 8-qt pot with nonstick spray. Add sausage to pot and cook over medium-high heat, stirring frequently to break up sausage, 6 minutes, or until browned. Pour off any fat. Stir in onion; cook 8 minutes, or until onion is browned, stirring frequently.

2. Stir in carrots, celery and garlic; cook 1 minute. Stir in beans, chicken broth and water. Bring to a boil. Reduce heat to low; cover and simmer 30 minutes, stirring occasionally.

3. Stir in tomatoes, squash, escarole and salt. Bring to a boil; reduce heat to low and simmer until squash is tender, 25 to 30 minutes. Season to taste with pepper.

Poker & potluck

When it's time for your special poker evening with the gang, make it a potluck. It's a great way for everyone to contribute and keep the costs down, too—that way you can save your dough for modest betting! Here are some tasty dishes for the perfect card party.

MAKES 4 CUPS

PREP: 20 MIN   COOK: 1 HR   CHILL: 2 HR

- ⅓   **cup olive oil**
- 1   **medium eggplant, cut into ½-in.-thick slices**
- 1   **tsp salt**
- 1   **large head garlic**
- 1   **box (8 oz) sliced mushrooms, chopped**
- 1   **zucchini (8 oz), cut into ¼-in. dice**
- 1   **jar (7 oz) roasted red peppers, rinsed, drained and chopped**
- 1   **container (8 oz) hummus**
- ¼   **cup fresh lemon juice (about 2 lemons)**

ROASTED VEGGIE DIP

1. Heat oven to 375°F. Brush a jelly roll pan with 1 Tbsp olive oil. Arrange eggplant in pan and brush both sides with 2 Tbsp oil. Sprinkle with ¼ tsp salt. Cut off top of garlic and wrap in a double layer of foil. Put in eggplant and garlic together. Roast the eggplant about 25 minutes, until tender. Let cool. Roast garlic until soft, about 1 hour.

2. Meanwhile, heat remaining oil in a large nonstick skillet over medium-high heat. Add mushrooms and ¼ tsp salt. Sauté until tender and liquid evaporates, about 6 minutes. Stir in zucchini and cook until tender, about 3 minutes. Turn into a large bowl.

3. Squeeze garlic cloves into a small bowl and mash with a fork. Finely chop eggplant. Add garlic, eggplant, red peppers, hummus, lemon juice and remaining ½ tsp salt to bowl with mushroom mixture. Stir well; cover and refrigerate 2 hours or up to overnight. Serve with pita chips.

SERVES 12

PREP: 15 MIN   ASSEMBLE: ABOUT 5 MIN

DRESSING

- 1 garlic clove, crushed through a press
- ½ cup olive oil
- ¼ cup Dijon mustard
- ¼ cup water
- 2 Tbsp balsamic vinegar
- ½ tsp salt
- ½ tsp freshly ground black pepper
- ½ cup flat-leaf parsley leaves

SALAD

- 1 large head romaine lettuce, cut into bite-size pieces
- 2 large carrots, shredded
- 3 celery stalks, sliced
- 4 tomatoes, cut into chunks
- 1 cucumber, peeled, halved lengthwise and sliced
- 2 cups shredded red cabbage
- 2 yellow bell peppers, diced
- 1 bunch radishes, thinly sliced
- ½ cup chopped red onion

SERVES 12

PREP: 10 MIN

- 1 Tbsp grated lime zest
- ½ cup lime juice (about 4 to 5 limes)
- 3 cups loosely packed fresh mint leaves
- ½ cup sugar
- 5 cups cranberry juice cocktail, chilled
- ¼ cup grenadine
- 3 cups club soda, chilled

  Ice cubes

  Garnish: mint sprigs

Note: Prepare the drink just before serving, as the mint will darken if made ahead.

LAYERED VEGGIE SALAD

1. Dressing: Combine garlic, oil, mustard, water, vinegar, salt and pepper in a blender. Blend until smooth; add the parsley and blend until chopped. Transfer the dressing to a bowl.

2. In a large straight-sided glass bowl, layer salad ingredients. Serve with dressing on the side.

CRANBERRY MOJITOS

1. In a blender, combine lime zest and lime juice, mint and sugar. Cover and pulse until mint is chopped.

2. Pour mint mixture into a large pitcher. Add cranberry juice and grenadine; stir to dissolve sugar. Gently stir in club soda. Pour over ice cubes in glasses. Garnish with mint sprigs.

INDIAN-SPICED SPINACH DIP

SERVES 12

PREP: 10 MIN (NOT INCLUDING PREPARING
VEGETABLE DIPPERS)

1   **ripe Hass avocado, halved
    and pitted**

1   **bag (5 oz) baby spinach**

2   **Tbsp lime juice**

1   **clove garlic, crushed with a press**

1   **tsp each curry powder and garam
    masala** *(see Note)*

¼   **tsp salt**

1   **cup nonfat plain Greek yogurt**

Garnish: diced plum tomato

Dippers: baby carrots; red, yellow and orange bell pepper strips; fresh fennel sticks; cucumber slices; radishes

1. Scoop flesh from avocado into food processor bowl; add spinach, lime juice, garlic, curry, garam masala and salt. Process until mixture is smooth.

2. Transfer mixture to a small bowl; stir in yogurt until blended. Garnish with diced tomato. Serve with raw vegetable Dippers.

Planning tip: You can make dip up to 3 days ahead and refrigerate.

Note: Garam masala is an Indian spice blend usually containing black pepper, chiles, cinnamon, cardamom and coriander. It may also include cloves, cumin, fennel, mace and nutmeg. Look for McCormick's garam masala where other spices are sold.

BAGNA CAUDA DIP & ROASTED VEGETABLES

SERVES 24

PREP: 5 MIN   COOK: 15 MIN (NOT INCLUDING
ROASTING VEGETABLES)

1   **cup extra-virgin olive oil**

1   **stick (½ cup) unsalted butter,
    softened**

2   **cans (2 oz each) flat anchovy
    fillets in olive oil, rinsed and
    drained**

6   **large cloves garlic, peeled and
    smashed with side of a knife**

2   **Tbsp lemon juice**

½   **tsp freshly ground pepper**

**Assorted roasted vegetables, such
    as potato wedges, cauliflower
    florets, butternut squash chunks,
    asparagus and beets** *(see Note)*

**Chunks of Italian bread, preferably
    semolina**

1. Combine oil, butter, anchovies, garlic, lemon juice and pepper in a food processor or blender and pulse until smooth.

2. Transfer mixture to a medium saucepan and cook over low heat 15 minutes, stirring occasionally (dip will separate; that's OK).

3. Pour into a fondue pot. Set pot over alcohol burner to keep warm. (You can also use a very small slow-cooker, set on low.) Serve with assorted roasted vegetables and chunks of Italian bread.

FYI: Bagna cauda (BAHN-yah KOW-dah) is a traditional Northern Italian sauce that includes anchovies and is served warm with vegetables for dipping. Anchovies add a wonderful depth of flavor not at all fishy or strong. If they're not your thing, omit them.

Planning tip: You can make dip through Step 2 up to 2 days ahead and refrigerate. Reheat before serving. Roast vegetables early in the day and reheat before serving. Assemble roasted beet and squash chunks on short bamboo skewers for easy dipping.

Note: Toss small potato wedges, cauliflower florets and butternut squash chunks with a little olive oil to coat; roast at 450°F for 45 minutes. Toss asparagus spears in olive oil; roast at 450°F 12 minutes or until crisp-tender. Wrap trimmed beets in foil and roast at 400°F for 1 hour or until tender; peel off skins after they cool.

FLIP-FLOPS CAKE

1. Heat oven to 350°F. You'll need a 13 x 9-in. baking pan coated with nonstick spray, bottom lined with wax paper and sprayed. You'll also need a sturdy serving surface about 20 x 16 in.

2. Prepare cake mix as directed for yellow pound cake, using pudding, water, eggs and oil. Pour batter into pan. Bake 35 to 40 minutes, until pick inserted into center comes out clean. Cool 10 minutes on wire rack. Remove from pan, peel off paper and cool completely.

3. With long serrated knife, trim top of cake horizontally to make level. Cut out 2 flip-flop shapes, each about 10½ x 5 in. Place on serving surface.

4. Tint ½ cup frosting light green. Transfer to small freezer ziptop bag with small hole snipped in one corner. Tint remaining frosting pink. Spread tops and sides of cakes with pink frosting.

5. Cut each rainbow sour belt lengthwise into two strips and arrange on cakes to make stripes, cutting as necessary to fit. Pipe decorative border of green frosting around top edges of cakes.

6. For straps, cut two 6½-in. pieces from red sour belts. Pinch two ends together on diagonal to attach. Trim remaining ends to round; place on top of one cake. Repeat to make strap for remaining cake.

7. Sprinkle serving surface with graham cracker crumbs. If desired, decorate with shell-shaped cookies and chocolates, gummy fish and starfish.

SERVES 12

BAKE: 35-40 MIN
DECORATE: DEPENDS ON SKILL LEVEL

EACH FLIP-FLOP MEASURES 10½ X 5 IN.

- 1 box (18.25 oz) yellow cake mix
- 1 box (3.4 oz) instant vanilla pudding mix
- 1 cup water
- 4 eggs
- ½ cup oil
- 2 tubs (16 oz each) white frosting
- Green and pink gel or paste food color
- 8 rainbow and 4 red sour belts candies

You'll also need: Graham cracker crumbs; shell-shaped cookies and/or chocolates; gummy fish and starfish

PERFECT PARTY CAKES

1. For large serving surfaces, you can use wax or parchment paper to cover a sheet of hard plastic foam (available at crafts and art-supply stores), doubled for extra strength if necessary, or a large cutting board.

2. Bake cakes up to 3 days ahead, cool and wrap airtight. Leave the decorating for another day.

3. If a cake requires two of the same size pan and you only have one, divide batter in half and bake one pan, leaving remaining batter covered at room temperature. Wash, dry and prepare pan. Bake remaining batter.

Planning tip: You can bake the cake up to 3 days ahead, wrap airtight and refrigerate. Frost and decorate up to 1 day ahead

DRAGON CAKE

1. Position oven rack just below center. Heat oven to 350°F. You'll need a greased and floured Classic Wonder Mold cake pan *(see Note)*.

2. Prepare one cake mix as directed using ¾ cup water and 2 eggs. Pour into pan; bake 50 to 55 minutes until toothpick inserted into center comes out clean. Cool 10 minutes. Remove from pan and cool on wire rack.

3. Clean, dry, and grease and flour pan. Repeat step 2 with remaining cake mix, water and eggs.

4. Prepare 1 batch Rice Krispies Treats as box directs, using 6 cups cereal, 1 bag marshmallows and 3 Tbsp butter. While still warm, shape into tail. Prepare remaining 2 batches using remaining cereal, marshmallows and butter. Shape about ⅔ of a batch for neck, and 1⅓ batches for head. If mixture becomes too firm while working, reheat for a few seconds in microwave, or keep warm in oven heated to 200°F. Let cool.

5. Spoon 2 Tbsp white frosting into small freezer ziptop bag. Snip hole in one corner. Tint 4 tubs frosting light green. Transfer 2 Tbsp light green frosting to another ziptop bag. Mix ¾ cup remaining frosting with ½ cup confectioners' sugar; tint yellow. Spoon into pastry bag fitted with large leaf pastry tip, or freezer ziptop bag with one corner snipped off. Mix remaining frosting with 1⅔ cups confectioners' sugar; tint dark green and spoon into pastry bag fitted with small star tip or freezer ziptop bag with one corner snipped off.

6. Cut a 1½-in.-wide vertical slice from the side of each cake. Sandwich cakes together along cut edges with thin layer of light green frosting. Using frosting to adhere, attach slices at each side of the rear cake to make hind legs. Attach neck and tail to cakes. Trim pointed ends from Bugles snacks and discard trimmings. Spread cakes, Rice Krispies Treats and Bugles with light green frosting. Attach Bugles (small end down) to dragon's head to make ears.

7. Pipe dark green frosting in spiky shapes all over neck, humps, hind legs and part of tail. Attach head to neck. Pipe stars over back of head and add a few warts on forehead, nose and tail. If using star tip, transfer remaining dark green frosting to freezer ziptop bag. Snip ½-in. hole in one corner. Pipe claws at front of each hind leg.

8. Pipe yellow scales behind each ear and a row of yellow spikes along back. Pipe white eyes and attach M&M's for pupils. With light green frosting, pipe eyelids and rings at top of each ear.

9. Cut 2½-in.-long pieces of strawberry Fruit by the Foot. Roll into cone shape, pinch ends and trim open end. Press into dragon's nostrils. Cut jagged pieces from Fruit by the Foot and attach under dragon's nose for flames.

MAKES 16 SERVINGS CAKE, 24 SERVINGS RICE KRISPIES TREATS

BAKE: ABOUT 2 HR
DECORATE: DEPENDS ON SKILL LEVEL

MEASURES 17 X 24 IN.

- **2 boxes (16 oz each) pound cake mix**
- **1½ cups water**
- **4 eggs**
- **18 cups Rice Krispies cereal from 2 (12-oz) boxes**
- **3 bags (10 oz each) marshmallows**
- **9 Tbsp butter**
- **7 tubs (16 oz each) white frosting**
- **Green and yellow gel or paste food color**
- **½ cup plus 1⅔ cup confectioners' sugar**

You'll also need: large leaf pastry tip and small star pastry tip *(see Note)*; 2 pieces Bugles corn snacks; 2 brown M&M's; 2 pouches Fruit by the Foot (1 strawberry, 1 Color by the Foot)

Note: Piping will go faster if you use Wilton or Ateco pastry tip #2010, which has 3 small star tips in one. Pastry tips, food colors and the Classic Wonder Mold cake pan (doll skirt–shaped pan) can be found at crafts and party stores, or at *wilton.com*.

MAKES 4

PREP: 10 MIN   BAKE: 8–10 MIN

3 **sheets frozen fillo dough,
thawed**

Butter-flavor cooking spray

½ **cup whipped cream
or topping**

1 **cup prepared vanilla pudding**

Sliced fresh strawberries

Confectioners' sugar

EASY STRAWBERRY NAPOLEONS

1. Heat oven to 350°F. Spray 1 sheet of fillo with butter-flavor cooking spray, then sprinkle with cinnamon sugar; top with a second sheet of fillo and cinnamon sugar.

2. Top with remaining sheet. Cut into 12 squares. Transfer to a baking sheet and bake 8 to 10 minutes until puffed and crisp. Fold whipped cream or topping into vanilla pudding.

3. For each Napoleon, top a pastry square with some pudding mixture and sliced berries. Repeat layer, then top with a pastry square. Dust with confectioners' sugar.

MAKES 2

PREP: 5 MIN

1⅓ **cups hulled strawberries**

  1 **cup strawberry ice cream,
plus more for 2 small scoops**

½ **cup milk**

Garnish: fresh berries

MILKSHAKE FLOATS

Blend strawberries, strawberry ice cream and milk until creamy and smooth. Pour into 2 tall glasses. Top each with a small scoop of ice cream and garnish with a berry.

SERVES 9

PREP: 15 MIN   CHILL: OVERNIGHT

  1 **lb hulled strawberries**

⅓ **cup sugar**

  1 **tsp almond extract**

1½ **cups thawed frozen
whipped topping**

  8 **oz mascarpone or
whipped cream cheese at
room temperature**

24 **Italian savoiardi cookies
(crisp ladyfingers)**

Garnish: semisweet chocolate

STRAWBERRY TIRAMISU

1. Purée berries with sugar and almond extract in blender. Fold thawed frozen whipped topping into mascarpone or whipped cream cheese until blended.

2. Trim 12 cookies so they fit into a 9-in-square pan or dish, side by side in 2 rows of 6, rows touching. Pour half the strawberry sauce over cookies, and then spread with half the cream mixture. Repeat with 12 more trimmed ladyfingers, arranging over cream layer; top with remaining strawberry sauce, then spread with remaining cream mixture.

3. Cover and refrigerate overnight. Grate semisweet chocolate over top of tiramisu. Cut into 9 squares.

PREP: 5 MIN   HEAT: ABOUT 2 MIN

- **1 cup heavy (whipping) cream**
- **1 lb bittersweet chocolate, finely chopped**
- **2 to 3 Tbsp coffee or hazelnut liqueur**

Dippers: fresh pear slices, crisp ladyfingers, dried apricots, marshmallows, strawberries

CHOCOLATE FONDUE

1. In a 4-cup microwave-safe bowl, heat cream on high just until steaming, about 1½ to 2 minutes.

2. Add the chocolate; let stand until shiny and softened, about 3 minutes. Add the liqueur and whisk until smooth.

3. Transfer to a ceramic fondue pot or ceramic chafing dish and keep warm over an alcohol burner or votive candle. (You can also use a very small slow-cooker, set on low.) Serve immediately with Dippers.

Planning tip: You can make fondue up to 3 days ahead and refrigerate. Reheat gently in microwave until hot and whisk to recombine just before serving. Rinse and dry fruit up to 2 hours before serving; keep at room temperature. Cut pears just before serving.

MAKES 44

PREP: 25 MIN   BAKE: 6–8 MIN PER BATCH
CHILL: AT LEAST 30 MIN FOR FILLING

MACAROONS

½ cup blanched whole almonds

1¾ cups confectioners' sugar

3 Tbsp unsweetened cocoa
   powder

Whites from 3 large eggs

Pinch of salt

2 tsp granulated sugar

FILLING

½ cup heavy (whipping) cream

2 Tbsp unsweetened cocoa
   powder

5 oz bittersweet or semisweet
   chocolate, finely chopped

1 stick (½ cup) unsalted butter,
   softened, cut up

Planning tip: The unfilled macaroons can be made 1 day ahead. Store airtight with wax paper between layers at room temperature. The filled cookies can be refrigerated airtight with wax paper between layers up to 2 days.

FRENCH CHOCOLATE MACAROONS

1. Position rack in middle of oven. Heat to 400°F. Line 2 large baking sheets with parchment paper or nonstick foil.

2. Macaroons: Pulse almonds and 1 cup confectioners' sugar in a food processor until finely ground. Add cocoa and remaining ¾ cup confectioners' sugar; pulse until well blended.

3. Beat egg whites and salt in a large bowl with mixer on medium-high speed until whites form soft peaks when beaters are lifted. Add granulated sugar and beat just until stiff peaks form when beaters are lifted. With a whisk or rubber spatula, gently fold in almond mixture. Transfer to a gallon-size ziptop bag. Snip ½ in. off a bottom corner and pipe 1-in.-diam mounds about 2 in. apart on prepared baking sheets.

4. Bake, 1 sheet at a time, 6 to 8 minutes, until tops look dry but macaroons are still slightly soft to the touch.

5. Transfer, still on parchment or foil, to barely dampened kitchen towels. Let cool 5 minutes. Carefully peel paper off macaroons and transfer to wire racks to cool completely.

6. Meanwhile, make **Filling:** Bring cream just to a boil in a medium saucepan over medium heat. Remove from heat; whisk in cocoa. Add chocolate and butter; whisk until melted and smooth. Cool to room temperature, then cover and refrigerate at least 30 minutes, or until firm enough to spread.

7. If piping Filling on cookies instead of spreading, transfer filling to a ziptop bag and snip ½ in. off a corner. Pipe or spread about 1½ tsp onto flat side of 1 macaroon. Top with another macaroon, flat side down, pressing together gently to form sandwich. Repeat with remaining macaroons.

TWIG WREATH
SHOWN ON PAGE 11
Skill Level: Beginner
Materials: 14-inch twig wreath form; black spray paint; scissors; dried or artificial silver dollar (lunaria) stems; hot-glue gun; black rubber spider; 8 inches of black rubber cord; 3 yards of 6-inch-wide black tulle ribbon; several feet of nylon monofilament.
DIRECTIONS: 1. Spray-paint all surfaces of wreath black; let dry. **2.** Cut stems to about 8 to 10 inches long; glue ends into wreath. **3.** Glue spider to one end of rubber cord. Glue other end of cord to back of wreath, near top, so spider hangs in center. **4.** Fold center of ribbon accordion-style to form about four 8-inch loops; wrap and tie end of ribbon around center to form bow. Glue ribbon to one side of wreath, near bottom. **5.** Loop monofilament through top of wreath; knot ends together at desired distance above wreath to form hanging loop.

TATTY CURTAINS
SHOWN ON PAGE 12
Skill Level: Beginner
Materials: Natural or tea-dyed cotton cheesecloth (we used Creepy Cloth from *orientaltrading.com*, which already has holes and tears); thumbtacks; scissors.
DIRECTIONS: 1. For door frame: Twist and tack center of cloth at top center of door frame. Loosely drape cloth along each edge of frame, tacking it in place at irregular intervals. For windows: Cut cloth into two pieces long enough to reach from window frame to floor. Tack each piece to window frame so raw edges meet in center. **2.** Use point of scissors to poke random holes and tears in cloth as desired.

POM-POM SPIDERS
SHOWN ON PAGE 12
Skill Level: Beginner
Materials (for each spider): Scissors; two 12-inch black bumpy chenille stems; hot-glue gun; one 2-inch black pom-pom; one 1½-inch black pom-pom.
DIRECTIONS: 1. Cut each chenille stem in half. Holding all 4 pieces together, twist in center to form 8 legs. **2.** Glue the 2-inch pom-pom over the twisted area to make the body. Glue the 1½-inch pom-pom

to the body to make the head. Bend legs as desired.

PERCHING BLACKBIRDS
SHOWN ON PAGE 12
Skill Level: Beginner
Materials: Black spray paint; large dry branches in varying lengths; assorted craft birds (plastic or feather); hot-glue gun; large vase.
DIRECTIONS: 1. Apply several coats of paint to branches and birds, letting dry after each coat. **2.** Glue birds to branches as desired. Place branches in vase.

MOLDINGS
SHOWN ON PAGE 12
Skill Level: Beginner
Materials: Ruler; black construction or wrapping paper; double-sided craft tape (low adhesive/repositionable); scissors; black thumbtacks (optional).
DIRECTIONS: 1. Measure area where element will be displayed. Enlarge the patterns at right to desired sizes (see *How to Enlarge Patterns*, page 143). **2.** Adhere pattern to black paper using double-sided tape; cut out pattern along outlines. **3.** Using double-sided tape or thumbtacks, attach element to wall as desired.

SKULL PLATES
SHOWN ON PAGE 13
Skill Level: Beginner
Materials: Clear glass plates; glass cleaner and paper towels; scissors; skull-print cotton fabric; foam paintbrush; clear decoupage medium; craft knife.
DIRECTIONS: 1. Thoroughly clean and dry plates. **2.** Cut fabric into circles with a diameter 1 inch longer than plates. **3.** Brush decoupage medium onto back of plate; center fabric, face down, on plate, smoothing from center out to remove air bubbles and folds. Let dry. **4.** Using craft knife, trim fabric along plate edges. **5.** Apply several coats of decoupage medium to back of plate, covering fabric edges; let dry after each coat.

BEETLES
SHOWN ON PAGE 13
Skill Level: Beginner
Materials: Black spray paint; plastic beetles; small paintbrush; opalescent craft paint in assorted colors.

DIRECTIONS: 1. Apply several coats of black paint to beetles, letting dry after each coat. **2.** Apply several coats of opalescent paint to the back of each beetle, letting dry after each coat.

SPOOKY SHADOWS
SHOWN ON PAGE 16
Skill Level: Beginner
Materials: Black window film for car windows (available at automotive stores); fine-point white oil paint marker; scissors; craft knife; cutting board.
DIRECTIONS: 1. Using photo as guide, draw designs with white marker onto film. Let dry. Cut out following inside edge of white marker lines. **2.** Following package instructions, apply film to windows.

JOLLY JACK-O'-LANTERNS
SHOWN ON PAGE 17
Skill Level: Beginner
Materials: Glass vases; measuring tape; paper; craft knife and scissors; spray glue; glue stick.
DIRECTIONS: 1. Measure vases and cut a piece of paper to wrap around the vase with a ¼-inch overlap in back. Turn paper over and lightly spray with glue over a covered surface. Smooth onto outside of vase. Use glue stick to attach overlap in back. (There should be no paper inside vase.) **2.** Using photo as guide, cut out eye, nose and mouth shapes from contrasting paper. Use glue stick to attach to vase.

CENTERPIECE
SHOWN ON PAGE 17
Skill Level: Intermediate
Materials: Large bread knife; 8-inch or 10-inch white plastic foam ball; paintbrush; FolkArt Acrylic Paint in Pumpkin Orange and Vivid Violet; tree branch; hot-glue and gun; scissors; craft foam in black, purple and yellow; lollipops; black, white and red tissue paper or fabric; black and white chenille stems; 1-inch foam brush; Fashion Brand Dimensional Shiny Fabric Paint in Black, Ultra Violet and Bright Yellow; string; googly eyes; yellow ½-inch rickrack; faux spiderweb.
DIRECTIONS: 1. Use bread knife to cut foam ball in half. Paint ball orange; let dry. **2.** Paint tree branch purple; let dry. Stick into center of orange ball and hot-glue to secure;

let dry. **3.** Bat: Using photo as guide, cut out wing shapes from craft foam. Wrap lollipop with black fabric or tissue. Twist black chenille stem around to hold and form legs. Glue on 2 small triangles of craft foam for ears. Decorate face with dimensional paint; let dry. **4.** Ghosts: Wrap lollipop with white square of fabric or tissue. Twist white chenille around neck of ghost to secure. Decorate face with dimensional paint; let dry. **5.** Spiders: Wrap lollipop with red fabric or tissue. Tie with string to secure. Cut 2 black chenille stems in half. Twist the 4 halves together in middle and glue to bottom of lollipop to form 4 legs on each side. Bend to shape. Glue on googly eyes. **6.** Glue rickrack to bottom edge of orange ball. Use dimensional paint to write on ball; let dry. **7.** Cut moon from yellow craft foam. Decorate with dimensional paint; let dry. Hot-glue to branch. Finish with faux spiderwebs.

GANG OF GHOULIES
SHOWN ON PAGE 17
Skill Level: Beginner
Materials: Red, purple and white balloons; black permanent marker; colored paper; scissors; double-stick tape; string or raffia.

DIRECTIONS: 1. Inflate balloon; knot. Draw features with marker, with knot at top of head. **2.** Cut out strips of paper to make arms and legs. Fold into accordion shapes for devil and skull, and attach to balloon with tape. Decorate with marker if desired. **3.** Hang from knotted end with string or raffia.

FELTED MUMMY DOLL
SHOWN ON PAGE 18
Skill Level: Intermediate
Materials: Sport-weight white wool yarn *(see Note)*; set of four size 10 double-pointed knitting needles; tape measure; fiberfill stuffing; yarn needle; 2 medium black buttons; 2 small blue buttons; 3 small gray buttons; embroidery floss: black, red; embroidery needle; washing machine and dryer.
Note: Use 100-percent wool yarn for best results; acrylics and blends will not felt properly. Exact gauge is not important for this project. Consult a knitting book if needed for additional knitting and felting tips.
DIRECTIONS: 1. Cast on 40 stitches, distributed across 3 needles, for head and body. Work in straight stitch until tube measures 4½ inches long. Next row, knit 2 stitches

together across row (20 stitches remain). Next row, knit all stitches. Next row, increase 1 stitch in each stitch (40 stitches on needles). Continue until tube measures 6 inches long, then cast off. **2.** Stuff body (use more stuffing in head than in body), then sew each end of tube shut. **3.** Cast on 20 stitches, distributed across 3 needles, for arm. Work in straight stitch until tube measures 6 inches long, then cast off. Make another arm in same manner. **4.** Stuff arms (use more stuffing in hands than in shoulders), then sew each end of tube shut. Sew arms to sides of body, just below neck. **5.** To make each leg, work same as for arms, but continue working until tube measures 8 inches long. Stuff (use more stuffing in feet than in thighs), then sew each end of tube shut. Sew legs to bottom of body. **6.** Layer black and blue buttons in pairs; sew to face for eyes. Sew gray buttons to front of body. **7.** Using black floss, sew a jagged row of straight stitches to face for mouth. Using red floss, sew a satin stitch heart on chest. **8.** To felt doll, wash in very hot water, then dry on high heat. Repeat several times as needed to shrink

doll and raise nap on wool. Wash and dry doll with towels to help fluff up the wool.

FELTED SKELETON DOLL
SHOWN ON PAGE 18
Skill Level: Beginner
Materials: Scissors; felt: white, black, red; pins; matching thread; sewing machine; scissors; fiberfill stuffing; hand sewing needle; 2 medium black buttons; 2 small green buttons; black embroidery floss; embroidery needle.

DIRECTIONS: 1. Enlarge skeleton doll pattern, below (see *How to Enlarge Patterns*, page 143). Cut head/body, arms and legs from white felt. **2.** Arrange body parts on black felt, placing them as desired and leaving space between sections. Pin. **3.** Stitch close to all edges of each body part to secure it to the black felt. **4.** Cut out a small heart from red felt; stitch heart to skeleton. **5.** Cut out black felt, leaving about 1 inch around body. **6.** Pin cutout piece onto another piece of black felt; cut second piece to match first. **7.** Sew pieces together close to edges, leaving an opening along one side. **8.** Stuff doll; finish sewing outer edge. **9.** Layer black and green buttons in pairs; sew to face for eyes. **10.** Using floss, sew a row of cross-stitches to face for mouth. Sew blanket stitches along edges of heart.

HANDS
SHOWN ON PAGE 18
Skill Level: Beginner
Materials (for one hand): Wood beads: 1 large, 10 small; C-clamps; electric drill and bits; wood spools: 6 large, 16 medium; foam paintbrush; white acrylic paint; small and medium wood spools; hot-glue gun; strong, thin twine; scissors.
DIRECTIONS: 1. Clamp large bead to work surface. Drill a hole straight through bead at a right angle to original hole, forming cross. Drill 2 more holes in bead, placing them to each side of new center hole and stopping when bit reaches original hole. This creates 5 holes for thumb and fingers over top of bead and one wrist hole at base. **2.** Paint all beads and spools; let dry. **3.** To make wrist section, glue 4 medium spools together end-to-end, keeping holes aligned. To make forearm section, glue 5 large spools

Felted Skeleton Doll
1 square = 1 inch

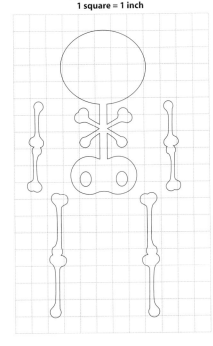

Mantel sides

Molding sides

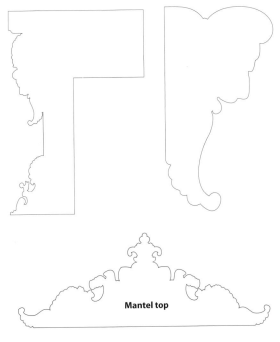

Mantel top

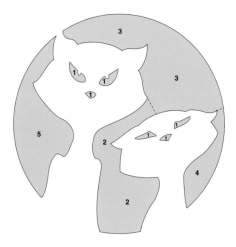

Dirty Duo

Treats

Tricks

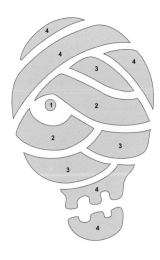

Bandaged Guy

Scary Hobgoblin

Pumpkin carving tips

FOR PROJECTS ON PAGES 20-21

■ Pick a pumpkin that's fresh and ready to last; avoid the ones with soft spots and nicks. Choose a pumpkin with smooth skin, rather than deep ridges, to make it easier to apply the pattern—more bumps equals more hassle.

■ Cut a circular lid into the pumpkin by carving a wide circle around the stem. Make sure it's at least big enough to put your fist through. Next, pull out as many seeds and stringy goo as you can by hand, then use a pumpkin or ice cream scoop to scrape the inside clean.

■ Use the flattest side of the pumpkin, even if it's the ugly side, for your design. This will make the carving process easier, and it won't show at night when lit.

■ Tape or pin the pattern onto your pumpkin (make sure the surface is dry so the tape will stick). Use a pumpkin poking tool, awl or nail to poke small, shallow holes through the paper, following the lines of the pattern. When all lines have been traced, remove pattern and save it for reference later.

■ Rip several tears about 3 inches apart all around the outside of the pattern before taping it down, if you're having trouble attaching the pattern. This will help you shape the paper to the pumpkin's rounded shape.

■ Poke the holes about ¼ inch apart—and even closer on complicated spots—after applying the patterns. The holes only need to just pierce the skin, or about ⅛ inch deep.

■ Rub flour, cornstarch or baby powder into the dots to make them stand out if you can't see the poked-out pattern.

■ Insert a carving saw (never use a knife) into a poked line. Always keep your noncarving hand away from the blade. Begin sawing out each section. Remember, saws don't twist and pumpkins don't give. To prevent your saw from breaking, saw curved areas carefully, gently turning the saw in the direction you wish to go while you continue to remove sections.

■ Hold your saw like a pencil and insert it at a 90-degree angle to the pumpkin's surface for a simple pattern.

■ Start with the smallest parts when carving. Carve the areas in the center of the pattern, then work your way out to the edges. Never rest your hand on a carved section; it might break.

■ Forget the top lid and carve an opening in the bottom if you're using a candle. Light the candle, then lower the pumpkin over it.

TOOLS OF THE TRADE

The right tools—flexible, sharp and sturdy—will make carving easier and yield the best results. Some may already be lurking in your kitchen or toolbox! Clean them thoroughly after each use and they'll last a lifetime.

KNIVES
Use a boning knife for cutting off the top and carving large areas; try a paring knife for the details. Sharpen both to a thin edge so they'll be easier to use and require less pressure when you cut.

SAW
A craft knife with a keyhole saw blade, available at home and crafts stores, is essential for carving the smallest details. In fact, you can carve most of your designs with this tool.

AWL
The sharp tip is perfect for transferring stencil designs onto the surface. A long nail or ice pick will also do the job.

CHINA MARKER OR GREASE PENCIL
Draw designs freehand before carving to ensure accuracy.

SCOOPING TOOLS
An ice cream scoop and a metal ladle will help remove the seeds and pulp from the inside of the pumpkin.

Continued from p. 137

together end-to-end, keeping holes aligned. **4.** To make fingers and thumb, cut 5 pieces of twine, each 3 times as long as the wrist and forearm total length. **5.** To make thumb, thread a small bead onto center of one piece of twine. Slip both ends through the remaining large spool, then through another small bead. **6.** To make each finger, thread a small bead onto center of each remaining piece of twine. For pinky, slip both ends through 2 small spools, then through another small bead. For middle finger, slip both ends through 4 small spools, then through another small bead. For index and ring fingers, use 3 small spools and assemble in same manner. **7.** Arrange fingers and thumb in correct order. Hold both twine ends together for each piece. Slip thumb twine through end hole in bead so ends extend through wrist hole. Slip index finger twine through second hole so ends extend through wrist hole. Slip twine from each remaining finger through holes in order so all ends extend through wrist hole. **8.** Hold all twine ends together. Slip all ends through wrist section, then forearm section. Knot ends together, leaving an inch or two of slack in twine. Trim ends. **9.** Pull twine knot to make the hand stretch out.

CONSTRUCTION-PAPER MANTEL
SHOWN ON PAGE 19
Skill Level: Beginner
Materials: Ruler; black construction or wrapping paper; double-sided craft tape (low adhesive/repositionable); scissors; black thumbtacks (optional).
DIRECTIONS: 1. Measure area where element will be displayed. Enlarge the patterns on page 137 to desired sizes (see *How to Enlarge Patterns*, page 143). **2.** Adhere pattern to black paper using double-sided tape; cut out pattern along outlines. **3.** Using double-sided tape or thumbtacks, attach element to wall as desired.

BLACK CAT PILLOWS
SHOWN ON PAGE 19
Skill Level: Beginner
Materials: Hand sewing needles; black thread; ½-inch black or pink button; black pillow (about 12 inches across in any fabric as desired); two ½-inch crystal buttons; white embroidery floss.
DIRECTIONS: 1. Thread a long needle with black thread; sew the ½-inch button to the center of the pillow, stitching all the way through and pulling the thread tight, forming the cat's nose. **2.** Sew crystal buttons above nose to make eyes. **3.** Thread an embroidery needle with 2 strands of floss. To make whiskers, make a small stitch on one side of the nose; tie thread ends together and trim to about 2 inches long. Make several more whiskers on each side of the nose in this way.

THANKSGIVING WREATH
SHOWN ON PAGE 32
Skill Level: Beginner
Materials: Glitter (copper, dark brown); small bowl; newspaper; grapevine wreath in desired size; spray adhesive; scissors; dried Chinese lanterns (from florist's shop or crafts store); hot-glue gun; 16 inches of floral wire; 4 yards of 2-inch-wide orange ribbon.
DIRECTIONS: 1. Mix glitters together in bowl. **2.** Cover work surface with 2 large sheets of newspaper (one for spraying with adhesive; one for sprinkling with glitter). Place wreath on one piece. Spray entire wreath with adhesive; move wreath to clean paper and sprinkle with glitter. Let dry. Pick up the second paper and pour glitter back into bowl. Place wreath on first paper to spray again, then place on second piece to add glitter again. When desired effect is achieved, let dry. **3.** Trim stems of lanterns to 2 inches; glue stems to cover wreath. **4.** To make hanging loop, fold wire in half and twist along length. Fold in half again and twist ends together to form loop. Twist ends around top of wreath. **5.** Cut ½ yard of ribbon for hanger and set aside. **6.** Cut remaining ribbon into 1-yard and 2½-yard pieces. Tie short piece into bow; place in center of long piece and tie that piece in a bow, holding small bow in place. Trim ribbon ends diagonally. **7.** Glue bow to lower side of wreath. **8.** Hang wreath using hanging loop. Slip reserved ribbon through top of wreath, then tuck ends behind mirror if attaching to one.

THANKFUL GARLAND
SHOWN ON PAGE 33
Skill Level: Beginner
Materials: Scissors; floral wire; dried Chinese lanterns (from florist's shop or crafts store); brown spray paint; small wood clothespins; small paintbrush; craft glue; copper glitter; parchment paper; metallic ink pens.
DIRECTIONS: 1. Cut floral wire to desired garland length, adding 10 inches for hanging. **2.** Starting 5 inches from one end, wrap wire around individual stems of lanterns, keeping lanterns in same direction. Garland should not be too full. Leave 5 inches of wire free at other end. **3.** Paint clothespins brown; let dry. **4.** Paint small amount of glue on one side of each pin; coat with glitter. Let dry. **5.** Cut parchment paper into 2x3-inch pieces. **6.** When guests arrive, have them use metallic pens to write what they are thankful for on parchment, then clip each paper onto garland.

LEAF CANDLES
SHOWN ON PAGE 33
Skill Level: Beginner
Materials: Small foam paintbrush; clear-drying decoupage glue; gold skeleton leaves (at crafts stores); candles in assorted sizes and colors.
DIRECTIONS: 1. Brush glue onto backs of leaves, then press onto candles. **2.** Let dry. Add more leaves as desired, keeping leaves away from top 1 inch of candle. Do not burn candles below tops of leaves.

THANKSGIVING NAPKINS
SHOWN ON PAGE 34
Skill Level: Beginner
Materials: Fine-point permanent marker; stencil plastic; craft knife and cutting mat; stencil adhesive; linen or cotton napkins in autumn colors; stencil brush; stencil paint for fabrics in autumn-leaf colors; iron.
DIRECTIONS: 1. Enlarge leaf patterns, right, to about 3 inches long (see *How to Enlarge Patterns*, page 143). Trace each onto a separate piece of stencil plastic. Using craft knife, cut out stencils. **2.** Spray back of stencil with adhesive; position on napkin near one corner, placing stem toward corner. **3.** Dip brush into paint, then pounce over stencil, starting at edges and working toward center. Remove stencil. **4.** Paint all napkins in same manner. When paint is dry, heat-set with iron, following paint manufacturer's directions.

BEADED NAPKIN RINGS
SHOWN ON PAGE 34
Skill Level: Beginner
Materials: Plain wood napkin rings; drill with ⅛-inch bit; sandpaper; small paintbrush; wood stain; soft cloth; 28-gauge gold wire, cut into 1-yard lengths; beads (leaf shapes in assorted colors, 3mm gold).
DIRECTIONS: 1. Drill holes in centers of napkin rings, making 6 holes evenly spaced. **2.** Sand rings. Brush on wood stain; wipe off excess and let dry. **3.** Wrap wire around ridge near one edge of ring, then thread end up through one hole.

Leaf Patterns

4. String a gold bead, then a leaf bead, onto wire, then slip wire back through gold bead and through same hole. **5.** Bring wire end through next hole and string beads in same manner. String beads through each hole in same manner. **6.** Wrap wire around ridge near other end of ring, then wrap wire end around wire inside ring to secure.

LEAFY TABLE RUNNER
SHOWN ON PAGE 35
Skill Level: Beginner
Materials: Scissors; thin cardboard; fabric marker; wool felt in assorted autumn-leaf colors; fabric glue; fine-point permanent brown marker.
DIRECTIONS: 1. Enlarge leaf patterns, page 139, to about 6 inches long (see *How to Enlarge Patterns*, page 143). Cut patterns from thin cardboard. **2.** Using fabric marker, trace leaves onto felt, tracing as many as needed for size of table. **3.** Arrange outer row of leaves to desired size of runner, mixing colors. Glue leaves together where they overlap. **4.** Fill in center of outline with leaves, overlapping as desired and gluing where leaves overlap. **5.** Using permanent marker, draw veins on leaves. **6.** If there are any extra leaves, use them as coasters.

CHAIR PLACE CARDS
SHOWN ON PAGE 35
Skill Level: Beginner
Materials: Scissors; thin cardboard; pencil; gold parchment paper; hole punch; metallic gold ink pen; 1/4-inch wide gold ribbon; acorn ornaments.
Note: You can use real acorns; just glue a large jewelry jump ring onto the top of each.
DIRECTIONS: 1. Enlarge leaf patterns, page 139, to about 4 inches long (see *How to Enlarge Patterns*, page 143). Cut patterns from thin cardboard. **2.** Trace patterns onto parchment paper, making one for each guest; cut out. **3.** Punch hole near stem of each leaf. **4.** Using metallic ink pen, write each guest's name on a leaf. **5.** Cut 1 yard of ribbon for each place card. Slip leaf, then acorn, onto center of ribbon; tie knot just above leaf. **6.** Tie ribbon ends in large bow on back of a chair to secure place card.

FALLING LEAVES
SHOWN ON PAGE 35
Skill Level: Beginner
Materials: Scissors; thin cardboard; pencil; gold parchment paper; small hole punch; gold cord or narrow ribbon; gold beads in assorted sizes.
DIRECTIONS: 1. Enlarge leaf patterns, page 139, to about 4 inches long (see *How to Enlarge Patterns*, page 143). Cut patterns from thin cardboard. **2.** Trace patterns onto parchment paper; cut out. **3.** Punch holes in leaves, starting 1/2 inch from tip and making holes about 1 inch apart along spine of leaf. **4.** Cut cord 4 inches longer than desired. Knot one end; slip on large bead, then thread other end in and out of leaf holes, adding beads as you thread. **5.** Knot cord at top of leaf. Make each leaf in this manner. **6.** Tie cords to curtain rod so leaves hang at different levels.

TREE SKIRT
SHOWN ON PAGE 54
Skill Level: Beginner
Materials: Scissors; 4 yards of main fabric, such as heavy cotton, upholstery fabric or felt, in 54-inch width (we used fabric from Calico Corners); pins; matching threads; sewing machine; chalk marking pencil; 1 yard of string; iron; yardstick; 2 yards of contrasting fabric.
DIRECTIONS: 1. Cut main fabric in half to make two 2-yard lengths. **2.** With right sides facing and raw edges even, pin pieces together along one long edge. Stitch from one edge to center (1-yard-long stitching line) with 1/2-inch seam allowance. **3.** Fold fabric in half crosswise so stitching line ends at fold. **4.** Tie string to pencil; pin other end of string to folded corner of fabric. Keeping string taut, use pencil to mark a quarter-circle along open edges of fabric. Using a 3-inch length of string and pencil in same manner, mark a quarter-circle at folded corner to form trunk opening. Leaving fabric folded, cut along both lines. **5.** Open out fabric; press seam open. **6.** Mark and cut contrast fabric into 3-inch-wide bias strips. Sew strips together end to end to make long trim strip. Trim seam allowances. **7.** Press under 1/2 inch on one long edge of trim.

Sew a row of long machine basting stitches near fold. **8.** Place skirt wrong side up. Pin unfolded edge of trim to outer edge of skirt, with trim wrong side up and trim ends even with each back opening edge of skirt. **9.** Sew trim to outer edge of skirt with 1/4-inch seam. Topstitch back opening edges and trunk opening 1/2 inch from edges. Clip into curved seam allowance and trim lower corners; turn trim to right side of skirt. Press lower edge of skirt. Turn under back opening edges and trunk opening 1/2 inch along stitch lines; press. **10.** Pull up long basted gathering stitches on trim so trim lays flat on skirt; press. Topstitch close to gathered edge of trim. **11.** Turn under pressed edges of back and trunk opening 1/4 inch; machine topstitch or hand hem close to folds to finish skirt.

TOPIARY BALLS
SHOWN ON PAGE 55
Skill Level: Beginner
Materials: 1-inch foam paintbrush; red acrylic paint; 3-inch plastic foam ball; hot-glue gun; red pistachios; egg cup or short candlestick holder.
DIRECTIONS: 1. Paint ball red; let dry. **2.** Place a dot of glue on closed end of pistachio; press onto ball. **3.** Continue gluing pistachios onto ball, placing them in rings and using smaller nuts to fill spaces. **4.** Display ball on egg cup or candlestick holder.

PARADE OF STOCKINGS
SHOWN ON PAGE 56
Skill Level: Intermediate
Materials: Cotton dish towels in assorted red-and-white prints; scissors; threads: red, white; sewing machine; cotton cord; pins; hand sewing needle; white buttons; iron.
DIRECTIONS: 1. Enlarge stocking pattern, opposite (see *How to Enlarge Patterns*, page 143). **2.** Fold a towel in half; cut stocking shape from both layers to make stocking front and back. Fold a contrasting towel in half for cuff. For curved cuff stocking (with button trim), cut four curved cuffs equal to width of stocking plus 1 inch by about 4 inches deep for front, back and linings. For striped cuff stocking, cut 1 cuff equal to width of stocking plus 1 inch by about 6 1/2 inches deep. For pleat-trim stocking, cut cuff equal to twice the width of stocking plus 1 inch x 1 1/4 inches deep from another contrasting towel. **3.** To make piping, cut 2-inch-wide bias strips from a contrasting towel. Sew strips together end to end with 1/4-inch seams to form bias strip long enough to go around outer edge of stocking, plus at least 4 inches; trim seam allowances. With right sides out, fold strip over cord; pin and stitch close to base of cord using a zipper foot to make piping. **4.** With right sides facing, pin piping along edges of small (2x3-inch) photos (printed sepia tone on regular computer paper—

Yuletide Gift Bag
1 square = 1 inch

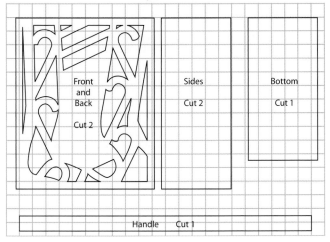

Front and Back — Cut 2

Sides — Cut 2

Bottom — Cut 1

Handle — Cut 1

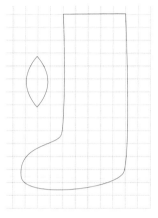

Felt Stocking
1 square = 1 inch

Stocking Doormat

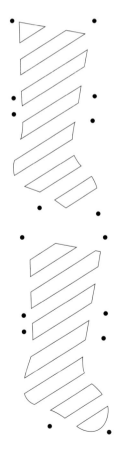

photo paper and photo-quality ink-jet papers are too thick), about 4 to 6 per ornament; stocking front, starting and ending at upper corners and keeping raw edges even. Baste close to base of piping using a zipper foot. **5.** Pin stocking front to back, with right sides facing and raw edges even. Stitch along basting lines on sides and lower edges using a zipper foot. Clip curves of seam allowance. **6.** For stocking with curved cuff, make additional contrast piping in same manner, making enough to go around sides and bottom edges of front and back cuffs, and around upper edge of stocking, plus at least 6 inches. Pin and baste piping to front and back cuffs in same manner, starting and ending at upper corners. Pin cuff linings to front and back cuffs, with right sides facing and raw edges even. Stitch along basting lines on all edges, leaving upper edge open. **7.** With stocking still wrong side out, pin remaining piping around upper edge in same manner, overlapping ends at back seam. Baste in same manner. Pin front and back cuffs to upper edge of stocking, with right side of cuff facing wrong side of stocking. Stitch ¼ inch from upper edge. Turn stocking right side out; turn cuffs to outside. Hand-stitch side edges of cuff together. Sew buttons along lower edge of front cuff. **8.** For stocking with striped cuff, fold cuff in half crosswise, with right sides facing and raw edges even; sew short end with ½-inch seam. Press seam open. Turn cuff right side out and fold in half lengthwise, wrong sides facing and raw edges even. Baste upper edges together. With stocking wrong side out, slip cuff around top of stocking, aligning raw edges and pin. Stitch cuff to upper edge of stocking with ¼-inch seam. Turn stocking right side out; turn cuff to outside. **9.** For stocking with pleat trim, fold trim in half crosswise, right sides facing, raw edges even; sew short end with ½-inch seam. Fold cuff in half crosswise, right sides facing, raw edges even; sew short end with ½-inch seam. Press both seams open. Turn cuff right side out and fold in half lengthwise, wrong sides facing and raw edges even. Baste raw edges together. Fold narrow pleats along raw edge of cuff so it fits along one raw edge of trim;

pin in place, raw edges even, right sides facing. Press pleats. Baste ¼ inch from edge. Fold under and press other long edge of trim ¼ inch. Then fold and press trim in half lengthwise, wrong sides facing, to cover raw pleated edge. Pin and stitch in the ditch to close trim. With stocking wrong side out, pin folded edge of trim to stocking top, with right side of cuff facing wrong side of stocking. Stitch cuff to stocking with ½-inch seam. Turn right side out. **10.** For all stockings, cut a 2x8-inch strip from any towel to make hanging loop. Fold strip in half lengthwise, with right sides facing and raw edges even. Stitch long edge with ¼-inch seam. Turn right side out; press. Stitch short ends together. Hand-stitch loop inside top of stocking.

PINECONE GARLAND
SHOWN ON PAGE 56
Skill Level: Beginner
Materials: Scissors; natural twine; hot-glue gun; small and medium pinecones; silk evergreen branches.
DIRECTIONS: 1. Cut twine 2 feet longer than mantel. **2.** Glue pinecones to twine, starting with medium cones and placing smaller cones to fill gaps. Leave a small amount of twine visible between cones. **3.** Drape evergreen branches on mantel, then arrange pinecone garland over branches.

CANDY CANE CONTAINER
SHOWN ON PAGE 57
Skill Level: Beginner
Materials: Vase or coffee can; wide red rubber bands; peppermint sticks; polyurethane sealer spray (optional).
DIRECTIONS: 1. Place rubber bands at different levels around vase. **2.** Unwrap peppermint sticks. Slip sticks under rubber bands, placing them side by side to cover vase completely. **3.** If desired, spray with several coats of polyurethane to prevent candy from becoming sticky.

WHITE BIRCH WREATH
SHOWN ON PAGE 58
Skill Level: Intermediate
Materials: 16- to 18-inch grape-vine wreath form; 5 pieces white birch bark, approximately 6x8 inches each; hot-glue gun; wire greening pins; floral wire;

6 artificial holly berry bush clusters with red berries; 2 stems green berries; 2 yards 1½-inch-wide wired sage-green ribbon.
DIRECTIONS: 1. Mold the five pieces of birch bark around the wreath form, with equal spaces between. Glue to back of wreath, and secure with greening pins. (Tip: If the bark is difficult to curve around wreath, soak in water for a few hours to make it even more pliable.) **2.** With floral wire, make a loop to hang the wreath and then attach it to the back of the form. **3.** Remove the berry clusters from the holly bushes (save leaves for another use) and glue between the birch sections. Mound the berries for a natural look, and cover the straight edges of the bark. Add a few green berries for accent. **4.** Make bow and glue to top center of wreath.

MEMORY WREATH
SHOWN ON PAGE 59
Skill Level: Beginner
Materials: 14-inch white plastic foam wreath base; white pipe cleaners; scissors; small (2x3-inch) photos (printed sepia tone on regular computer paper—photo paper and photo-quality inkjet papers are too thick), about 4 to 6 per ornament; jar all-in-one sealer (such as Mod Podge); paintbrush; 6 to 8 champagne-colored Christmas balls, 2½-inch diameter (or another light color so it won't show through the photos); hot-glue gun; wired Christmas balls in shades of copper: about 35 clusters of 1-inch balls, about 75 to 100 individual 1½-inch balls; 5 yards 1½-inch-wide copper-colored sheer ribbon.
DIRECTIONS: 1. Use white pipe cleaners to make a hanging loop at the top of the wreath. **2.** Cut photos. With all-in-one sealer and paintbrush, paste onto large ornaments, overlapping edges to completely cover the surface. When surface is covered, apply another coat of sealer over entire ornament. **3.** Secure large ornaments evenly around wreath form. Fill in with clusters of 1-inch and 1½-inch Christmas balls to create a mounded effect. **4.** Cut copper ribbon into 6 to 8 strips, about 4 to 6 inches each. Weave between ornaments to fill bare spots, securing with hot glue. Finish with bow at top.

GIFT BOX WREATH

SHOWN ON PAGE 59

Skill Level: Beginner

Materials: Wrapping paper in assorted colors; scissors; tape; small gift boxes; ribbon remnants; foam paintbrush; craft glue; small plastic foam shapes: balls, bells, stars; glitter in assorted colors; medium plastic foam balls; fabric remnants; beaded pins; several yards of 2-inch-wide silver ribbon; plastic wreath form or ring; small glass ball ornaments.

DIRECTIONS: 1. Wrap boxes with gift wrap; tie ribbon bows around each. **2.** Brush glue on small foam shapes, then roll in glitter; let dry, then shake off excess. **3.** Cut two circles of fabric for each medium foam ball, making each circle large enough to go halfway around each ball. Smooth and glue fabric to each half of each ball. Wrap and pin ribbon over seam. Wrap and pin additional ribbon on each ball as desired. **4.** Glue one end of silver ribbon to wreath form; wrap and glue ribbon to cover form in overlapping layers. **5.** Glue largest gift boxes to front of wreath, allowing them to extend past edges. Glue glitter and fabric ornaments and glass balls to fill spaces between boxes.

HYDRANGEA WREATH

SHOWN ON PAGE 59

Skill Level: Intermediate

Materials: 16- to 18-inch grapevine wreath form; green pipe cleaners or floral wire; 2 stems preserved natural hydrangea; 1 stem preserved green hydrangea; hot-glue gun; 5 pomegranates (dried); 4-inch wired wooden pics; 1 bunch berried twigs; 1 bunch green millet (dried); 40 stems dried red roses; 8 to 10 cinnamon sticks (4 to 6 inches long); 1 bunch green pimentina (dried small green flower); 1 bunch mini-pinecones on wires; 1 cluster acorns (dried).

DIRECTIONS: 1. Use green pipe cleaner or floral wire to make a hanging loop on back of wreath. **2.** Separate hydrangea into small clusters. Insert stems into vine wreath, adding a small dab of hot glue if needed to secure. **3.** Push a wooden pic into the back of each pomegranate and

secure with a drop of hot glue; position equally around wreath, securing each one in place. **4.** At the top of the wreath, create a focal point by wiring in berried twigs and green millet. Add the dried roses in clusters. Divide the cinnamon sticks equally and wire onto form in 2 clusters. **5.** Fill in bare spots with remaining small decorative elements and finish with the cluster of acorns.

HOLIDAY DOVES

SHOWN ON PAGE 62

Skill Level: Beginner

Materials: Small paintbrush; craft glue; white craft dove; white glitter; white feathers; small white clothespin (from crafts stores).

DIRECTIONS: 1. Brush thin layer of glue over dove's body; sprinkle with glitter. Let dry. **2.** Glue feathers to dove's tail, adding them one at a time and working in a ring around tail. **3.** Glue clothespin to foot area of dove so ornament can be clipped on tree.

NATURE'S ORNAMENTS

SHOWN ON PAGE 62

Skill Level: Beginner

Materials: Small paintbrush; craft glue; Christmas ornament balls; glitter in assorted colors; small crafts insects, such as ladybugs and dragonflies.

DIRECTIONS: 1. Brush thin layer of glue onto ornament; sprinkle on glitter. **2.** Brush thin layer of glue onto areas of insects; sprinkle on glitter to match ball's original color. Apply glitter to remaining areas of insects in same manner. **3.** Glue insects to ornaments.

SWIRLY ORNAMENTS

SHOWN ON PAGE 62

Skill Level: Beginner

Materials: Pencil; Christmas ornament balls; small paintbrush; craft glue; glitter (green, blue, purple, silver).

DIRECTIONS: 1. Lightly mark desired glitter pattern on ornaments. **2.** Brush thin layer of glue on each line; sprinkle on silver glitter. **3.** Brush glue onto one section of ornament between silver lines; sprinkle on colored glitter and let dry in same manner. **4.** Add glitter to each section of ornament in same manner.

RHINESTONE ORNAMENTS

SHOWN ON PAGE 62

Skill Level: Beginner

Materials: Christmas ball ornaments in assorted sizes; chalk marking pencil; hot-glue gun; rhinestones in assorted sizes.

DIRECTIONS: 1. Lightly mark pattern for rhinestones on ball. **2.** Starting in center, glue large rhinestone to ornament. **3.** Continue adding rhinestones, working from largest stones near center to smallest stones at points. Let dry.

CRYSTAL FLOWER NAPKIN RINGS

SHOWN ON PAGE 63

Skill Level: Beginner

Materials: 25mm x 18mm oval faceted acrylic gems in assorted colors; hot-glue gun; 20mm flat-back faceted acrylic gems in assorted colors; 1½-inch diameter gold rings.

DIRECTIONS: 1. Arrange 4 oval gems in flower shape, with narrow ends in center; glue. **2.** Glue another 4 gems on top of this layer, alternating the petals. **3.** Glue a flat-back gem in center. **4.** Turn flower over; glue edge of ring to center of flower.

YULETIDE GIFT BAG

SHOWN ON PAGE 64

Skill Level: Beginner

Materials: Scissors; 1 yard of red felt; ½ yard of paper-backed fusible web; iron; press cloth; transfer paper; tracing wheel; pins; red embroidery floss and embroidery needle or red thread and sewing machine.

DIRECTIONS: 1. Cut felt in half. Following manufacturer's directions, fuse web onto one piece of felt. **2.** Peel off paper backing. Place other piece of felt on top of web; fuse layers together, using press cloth to protect iron. Let cool. **3.** Enlarge gift bag pattern, page 140 (see *How to Enlarge Patterns*, page 143). Transfer all pattern markings onto felt to cut one front, one back, two sides, one bottom and one handle. **4.** Cut out each piece, using small pointed scissors to cut out smaller sections on bag front and back. **5.** Pin sides to bottom at short ends; hand stitch using blanket stitch or machine stitch. **6.** Pin front to one edge of side and bottom section;

stitch in same manner. **7.** Pin back to other edge of side and bottom section; stitch in same manner. **8.** Pin ends of handles to sides so they overlap 1 inch; stitch in place.

STOCKING DOORMAT

SHOWN ON PAGE 64

Skill Level: Beginner

Materials: Doormat; scissors; pencil; large sheet of kraft paper; blue painter's tape; spray paints (red, green).

DIRECTIONS: 1. Enlarge doormat patterns, page 141 (see *How to Enlarge Patterns*, opposite) to fit mat. Cut out motifs; trace outlines onto kraft paper. Cut out templates from kraft paper, cutting 2 each of the red and green templates. **2.** Tape red templates onto mat, spacing as desired and covering all areas of mat except those that will be painted red. **3.** Spray red paint over desired areas, including outer border, starting at edge of paper and working toward center. Remove template; let dry. **4.** Tape green template over mat, covering all areas of mat except those that will be painted green and aligning templates over red areas. Use large dots to help align pieces properly. **5.** Spray green paint in same manner.

NOEL GARLAND

SHOWN ON PAGE 65

Skill Level: Beginner

Materials: Children's cotton socks (old or new in assorted sizes); red fabric dye (see package for other materials needed); thread (red, white); hand-sewing needle; red ball fringe; white trims (such as buttons, ribbons and charms); scissors; 2 yards of ½-inch-wide red ribbon.

DIRECTIONS: 1. Wash and dry socks. Follow dye manufacturer's directions to mix dye. Dye socks according to package directions; rinse and dry. **2.** Sew ball fringe along cuffs of some socks. Turn down cuffs; stitch in place. **3.** Sew assorted white trims to fronts of socks, including cuffs. **4.** Cut red ribbon to desired garland length, adding several inches at each end for hanging. Starting in center, sew socks to garland, spacing them evenly and stopping several inches from each end.

FLOOR PILLOWS
SHOWN ON PAGE 65
Skill Level: Beginner
Materials: Old Christmas stockings; fiberfill stuffing; thread to match stockings; hand sewing needle.
DIRECTIONS: 1. Fill stockings with stuffing, pushing it well into toe area and being careful to keep stocking shape. **2.** Hand stitch upper edge of stocking shut.

DRINKING GLASSES
SHOWN ON PAGE 120
Skill Level: Beginner
Materials: Set of glasses with straight sides; stickers (we used ¾-inch and 1-inch dots); basic etching supplies (see *The Essentials,* this page).
DIRECTIONS: 1. Clean and dry glasses thoroughly. **2.** To create dotted glasses, apply dot stickers to the outside of the glass, placing them where you want the glass to remain clear (the remainder of the glass will appear frosted). **3.** For striped glasses, cut painters tape into ⅛-, ¼- and ½-inch-wide strips about 1 inch longer than the height of the glass. Apply tape strips to each glass so that the ends extend above and below the sides. Space strips according to where you want the glass to remain clear. **4.** Using the orange stick, burnish the edges of the stickers or tape so they adhere to the glass. Place glasses on the covered cookie sheet. **5.** Put on gloves, then apply a thick layer of etching cream to the entire outside surface of the glass, covering the stickers or tape. **6.** Apply gobs of cream, as opposed to using smooth strokes, so that brush marks don't show on the finished glass. Allow cream to set for about half an hour, or as long as your test indicates (see "Etching Cream" in *The Essentials,* right). **7.** Rinse the item under running water, then wash with soap. Peel off the stick-ons. Use glass cleaner to remove all cream and glue residue from the surface.

PITCHER
SHOWN ON PAGE 121
Skill Level: Intermediate
Materials: Glass pitcher; artwork of your making (see "Juice" pattern,

above); scissors; clear adhesive shelving paper (from hardware or home stores); basic etching supplies (see *The Essentials,* right).
DIRECTIONS: 1. Clean and dry pitcher thoroughly. **2.** Print out artwork and enlarge to fit your pitcher. Tape the pattern inside the pitcher, making sure it is straight **3.** Cut a piece of shelving paper 2 inches larger than the pattern on all four sides. Peel off the paper backing and adhere the plastic onto the outside of the pitcher, centered over the pattern. Smooth the plastic from the center out to remove any air bubbles. Use the craft knife to cut out each letter, working from the corners to the center. Peel off the letters, leaving the rest of the plastic in place. **4.** Using the orange stick, burnish the edges of the plastic, paying particular attention to the edges of the letters. Place the pitcher on the covered cookie sheet. Put on gloves, then apply a thick layer of etching cream over the plastic, keeping the cream away from the outer inch of the plastic and covering the letters well. Continue from Step 6 of the Drinking Glasses project, left.

CAKE DOME
SHOWN ON PAGE 121
Skill Level: Advanced
Materials: Glass cake dome; basic etching supplies (see *The Essentials,* right); paisley artwork (see pattern, right); pen; clear adhesive shelving paper (from hardware or home stores); scissors; adhesive binder-hole reinforcements.
DIRECTIONS: 1. Clean and dry cake

dome thoroughly. Apply painters tape along its upper and lower edges to mark off the center-etched band. **2.** Print out the artwork and enlarge it to the desired size. Trace the paisley pattern as many times as needed onto the shelving paper. Punch holes into paper paisleys as desired; save the cutout centers and use them to create dots on some of the other paisleys. Use the craft knife to cut out each motif along the outlines. Peel off the paper backing and adhere the plastic onto the dome, spacing motifs evenly. Smooth the plastic from the center out to remove any air bubbles. **3.** Cut the reinforcements in half and apply them along the edges of some of the

Paisley

paisley motifs for a scalloped effect; place whole ones between motifs. **4.** Using the orange stick, burnish the edges of the plastic and painters tape. Place the dome on the covered cookie sheet. Put on gloves, then apply a thick layer of etching cream over the plastic, working up to the edges of the tape and covering the motifs well. Continue from Step 6 of the Drinking Glasses project, left.

THE ESSENTIALS:
BASIC ETCHING SUPPLIES
Cookie sheet, tin foil: Cover a large, old cookie sheet with tin foil to create a work surface.
Craft knife, cutting mat: Use these to cut shapes from adhesive sheets and painters tape.
Etching cream: We used Armour Etch cream for all of these projects. You can find it at crafts stores or *etchworld.com* (800-872-3458); it's available solo or in kits that include many of the other supplies you'll need. You may want to test the effect of cream on a remnant of glass before working on your project; the time recommended on the package may not be enough for the look you want.
Glass cleaner: Use cleaner to ensure that the surface is completely clean before you start your project and be sure to rinse all residue off the glass. Also, use the cleaner after the glass has been etched and thoroughly rinsed under running water.
Hole punch: Handy for cutting smaller dots.
Orange stick: Steal one from your manicure supplies; these wooden sticks, with their tapered ends, are perfect for burnishing the edges of your stickers and tape so the etching cream doesn't seep underneath.
Painters tape: Use to create patterns and secure artwork to glass.
Rubber gloves: The etching cream is made with a strong chemical, so be sure to keep your hands protected!
Soft paintbrushes: Use camel-hair or other nonsynthetic paintbrushes with etching cream. A ½-inch-wide brush is good for many basic projects, but a larger brush will come in handy for coating broad areas.

HOW TO ENLARGE PATTERNS
Using a colored pencil and ruler, mark a grid on the pattern by connecting grid lines around the edges. On a sheet of paper, mark a grid of 1-inch squares (or size given), making the same number of squares as on the pattern. To do this, use graph paper with 1-inch squares. In each square, draw the same lines as in the corresponding square on the pattern. Another way to enlarge is by using a photocopier.

Many, many thanks to all the talented designers and stylists whose projects we included in this book. Without their extraordinary work, this book would not be possible.

Front cover, clockwise from top left: Alan Richardson, Michael Partenio, Mary Ellen Bartley, Mary Ellen Bartley. Back cover, from top to bottom: Deborah Ory, Mary Ellen Bartley.
p. 1: John Gruen; p. 2: Mary Ellen Bartley; p. 6, from top to bottom: Deborah Ory, Michael Partenio, Charles Schiller; pp. 8, 10: Deborah Ory; p. 11: Susan McWhinney (top and left), Deborah Ory (right); pp. 12–13: Susan McWhinney; pp. 14–15: Deborah Ory; pp. 16–17: John Gould Bessler; pp. 18–19: Susan McWhinney; pp. 20–21: Deborah Ory; p. 22: Stephanie Foley; pp. 23–24: Wendell Webber; pp. 26, 29: Mark Ferri; pp. 30, 32–35: Deborah Ory; pp. 36, 38: Kate Sears; p. 39: Antonis Achilleos; p. 40: Kate Sears; p. 43: Mark Ferri; pp. 44–48, 50,–51: Kate Sears; p. 52: John Gruen; pp. 54–56: Michael Partenio; p. 57: Michael Partenio (top and bottom left), John Gruen (top right); pp. 58: Susan McWhinney; p. 59: Susan McWhinney (top and center right), John Gould Bessler (bottom left); pp. 62–65: Deborah Ory; p. 66: Alexandra Grablewski; p. 68: Jacqueline Hopkins; p. 69: Alexandra Grablewski; p. 70: Charles Schiller; pp. 72–75: Susan McWhinney; p. 76: John Uher; p. 77: Shaffer Smith; p. 78: Mary Ellen Bartley; pp. 80, 82: John Uher; p. 84: Mary Ellen Bartley; p. 86: Dasha Wright; p. 87: Mary Ellen Bartley; p. 88: Charles Schiller; p. 89: Mary Ellen Bartley (top), Alison Gootee (bottom left), Antonis Achilleos (bottom right); pp. 90, 92–93: Anastassios Mentis; p. 94: Mary Ellen Bartley; p. 96: Charles Schiller; pp. 97–98: Mary Ellen Bartley; pp. 100, 102: Iain Bagwell; p. 103: Anastassios Mentis; pp. 104–105: Iain Bagwell; pp. 106–107: Alan Richardson; p. 108: Ken Hayden; pp. 110–111: Joe Schmelzer; p. 112: Mark Thomas; pp. 114, 116: Joe Schmelzer; p. 117: John Blais; p. 118: Joey De Leo; pp. 120–121: John Gould Bessler; pp. 122, 124–125: Joey De Leo; p. 126: Wendell Webber; pp. 128, 131: Alan Richardson; pp. 132–133: Mary Ellen Bartley; p. 134: Wendell Webber; p. 135: William Meppem.